# LIGHT ON THE PATH TO S|

## ADDITIONAL ARTICLES I

by

Ray del Sole

LIGHT ON THE PATH TO SPIRITUAL PERFECTION

ADDITIONAL ARTICLES I

Attention

Please regard that you take the responsibility for all exercises, experiments and advices you do or follow in this book. All warnings of spiritual teachers, especially by Franz Bardon, Indian Yogis and me should be taken serious. Spiritual training is an art and science and not something to play with or for curiosity. Spiritual development takes years, whole life times, many incarnations indeed. As you are an eternal being you have time enough to proceed step by step keeping the balance in all aspects.

I dedicate this book to Daisy. She is the perfect expression of the God given joy of life. She is an inspiration for everyone who meets her. She has won my heart at first sight.

Ray

## FOREWORD

I have not expected to become an author but somehow it has happened. I have also not expected that I would write so many books. Life often provides things which we do not expect but which simply happen or manifest. In fact I have no time to write books but I did it nevertheless. In fact I wanted to write only one or two books if ever but I haven't stopped so far. Obviously there are still enough topics on my mind which somehow wants to be written down and published. I hope you can forgive me.

Ray del Sole

# Content

The wire dancer and the abyss....................................................9

Statement about the speech of the Pope .....................13

The bullwhip of Mammon .........................................17

The Hermetic Study Circle........................................21

A Dynamic Meditation Technique...............................24

The magic of making plans .......................................25

Enhanced technique for autosuggestion ......................28

Magical investments ...............................................29

Saturation and perfection........................................30

Question about a simple way to learn magic.................32

Technique for Karma Yoga ......................................35

Human wishes versus divine aims .............................37

Some words about the nature of Franz Bardon...............38

Good advice by Eric Idle .........................................40

Q: What can I do when Bardon´s teachings seem to be too difficult for practice? ...............................................43

Hell and Mother Holle.............................................45

Beyond good and bad..............................................46

Experiment...........................................................47

Using mantras ......................................................47

Hypnosis and parapsychology ..................................51

Sensing animals ....................................................52

Shifting on the meta level .......................................54

THE PROCESS OF MASTERING NEW ABILITIES IN MAGIC ........................56

DISSOLVING OF BLOCKADES IN AUTOHYPNOSIS ....................................60

QUESTION: THOUGHT CONTROL AND MOTIVATION ............................62

SPACE CLEARING .........................................................................63

FAMILY AND KARMA INHERITANCE ...................................................64

THE YEAR 2012 ........................................................................69

LAWS, JUSTICE AND ORDER ...........................................................71

SPECIAL TECHNIQUE FOR AUTOHYPNOSIS .........................................73

HELP FOR VISUAL IMAGINATION ......................................................74

TENSION AND POWER....................................................................75

THE MAGIC OF RESOURCES ............................................................76

LOVE – A MASTER KEY .................................................................79

THE HAWK WHO LIVED AMONG THE PIGEONS ....................................79

THE WORK OF LIGHT AND DARKNESS ...............................................81

PRIVILEGES.................................................................................82

BOOK RECOMMENDATION..............................................................83

PROGRESSION, IMAGINATION AND MASTERSHIP .................................84

SOMETHING CURIOUS ...................................................................87

MENTAL HEALTH .........................................................................88

ABOUT EGOISM...........................................................................90

HEALING TECHNIQUE WITH AKASHA.................................................91

SOMETIMES… .............................................................................92

STUDY ABOUT SHEEP ...................................................................94

PROGRESS BOOSTER FOR MAGICAL DEVELOPMENT.............................94

A CASE OF KARMA ........................................................... 97

DIRECT KNOWLEDGE .......................................................100

THE DIVINE GARDEN........................................................100

THE BLACK TOURMALINE....................................................101

SPIRITUAL PROCLAMATION ..................................................103

TRAVELING INTO TRANCE ...................................................106

WHERE BARDON´S SYSTEM LEADS TO...........................................109

SPECIAL SELF-HEALING TECHNIQUE .........................................112

THE PROBLEM OF BARDON´S TRAINING .......................................113

MERGING WITH THE SPHERES ...............................................115

DISCUSSING MASTERSHIP AND ENLIGHTENMENT ...............................117

ENVIRONMENTAL POLLUTION IN BARDON FORUMS..............................118

SATANISTS AND PSYCHOPATHS ..............................................122

SPIRITUAL WORK AND HYPNOSIS ...........................................123

ABOUT DISCUSSIONS ......................................................124

PROBLEMS OF MANKIND AND THEIR SOLUTION ...............................127

SPECIAL TECHNIQUES FOR TARGET-IMAGINATION ............................128

PAST-LIFE-THERAPY: TRAVELING THROUGH SPACE & TIME .................130

TRADITIONAL KABBALAH VERSUS BARDON´S COSMIC LANGUAGE ........131

CIRCLE TECHNIQUE FOR DISSOCIATION .....................................133

GAMES FOR TRAINING ....................................................134

AIR ELEMENT FOR REGENERATION .........................................135

THE UNIVERSAL SOLVENT AND REMEDY CALLED LOVE ........................136

ABOUT PAST-LIFE-THERAPY ...............................................138

THE PERSONAL GOD ....................................................... 139

HEALING AND KARMA.................................................... 141

THE CHALICE OF FORGIVENESS ..................................... 142

DISEASES OF THE PRESENT LIFE ..................................... 143

HEALING OF THE DECEASED ........................................... 144

BALANCING OF AIR AND EARTH ..................................... 146

THREE MAIN ASPECTS OF HEALING ................................ 147

MIND PROGRAMMING.................................................... 148

BREATHING EXERCISE ................................................... 150

ADDITION FOR INTROSPECTION ..................................... 151

INDIRECT HEALING TECHNIQUE...................................... 152

THE DEVELOPMENT OF THE SELF-AWARENESS .................. 154

THE TRUE PROBLEM OF MANKIND ................................... 155

THE MYSTERY OF FULLNESS ......................................... 157

ABOUT PARAPSYCHOLOGY............................................. 158

THE MATERIALISTIC DIMWITS - IGNORANT, ARROGANT AND UGLY........ 159

THE HOLISTIC HEALING TREATMENT ............................... 163

TRAVELING THROUGH TIME AND SPACE ........................... 166

Epilogue.................................................................... 168

contact .................................................................... 169

Index ....................................................................... 171

# THE WIRE DANCER AND THE ABYSS

In the last days I have been thinking about different "spiritual" traditions, their leaders, their teachings and their followers. Over and over again there were a few eye-catching points, - dangerous points.

For good reasons the old spiritual masters said that the path is as fine as the sharp edge of a knife. You can also say that a spiritual seeker has to make the path like a wire dancer above the abyss. So why do spiritual masters say something like this while others say that all ways lead to the same aim? It sounds like a contradiction. The point here is the question regarding the kind of path you want to go. The straight path from A to B is the fine line across the abyss which you have to master like an artist, - like a wire dancer. All other paths are quite relative with no statement about the needed time, the dangers and the loop ways you will have to take. It is the "I couldn't care less" attitude. It cannot be in the interest of a seeker to take risks, dangers, torture, darkness, endless time and effort to reach his spiritual aims but there are people who do not care at all if someone is misled or walking straight to the edge of the abyss. These people, - equal if they call themselves "masters" or if they are "students" lack of compassion and I would call them simply human assholes. Compassion for all beings and especially for brothers and sisters on the path is a spiritual virtue, a clear sign of spiritual maturity and real progress. Certainly not every seeker is receptive for higher teachings, for warnings or advice but one should try to give him the right orientation. Love is the law and not dullness or apathy.

So why behave so called "spiritual" people in this careless way? Because of ignorance, wrong teachings, misunderstanding of teachings and bad, unrefined characteristics. So called teachers or leaders of certain traditions do this as well because of ignorance and misunderstandings but also because of major imbalances of mind and soul, - psychic illness. Such imbalances are results from following the wrong path, from disregarding higher laws and from egoistic tendencies. I repeat and emphasize this, - there are not only a few "spiritual leaders" of esoteric traditions which suffer unconsciously from real mental and psychic imbalances, from wrong philosophies, from wrong, one-sided training. Indeed such leaders should have undergone psychotherapy instead of misleading other people. The tragedy is that those people haven´t noticed how they left the right path, how they have lost themselves in darkness and delusion, in extremes, how they have moved away from the center of life. This is all very sad, - sad for themselves and sad for their followers and for both it is very hard to escape the darkness of the abyss and to get back into the light.

When you do studies on such leaders you can examine very often that the tragedy has started very early already with a wounded soul, with traumatic happenings or with bad life circumstances. Instead of healing the wounds of their souls, instead of analyzing their situation such leaders kept their wounds and imbalances by and built up whole philosophies together with "secret" knowledge on their bad experiences. So certainly this cannot be the truth or wisdom, - this is just extreme and ill.

There is a big heap of "esoteric" rubbish, of not reflected, misunderstood teachings, half-truths, prejudices, fanaticism, darkness and pure evil. People are often easily trapped in as most people do not reflect and think much on their selves. Unfortunately most people lack of knowledge and the energy to use their brains. This is also valid for so called intelligent or intellectual people. This is all very sad.

Nice traps are for example the idea that everything is relative. This is already a contradiction in itself. Wrong is also to proclaim that light and darkness are of the same quality and that light depends on darkness. When you look on the surface of the material world then you might think that only material laws are at work without any love and grace, without a divine being. If you think so you should improve your perception or maybe clear your perception filter. A great delusion is also to believe that everything is a matter of karma and prediction, - that when you kill or misuse someone he is responsible because of his "victim-karma" and so you are free of any responsibility. Prediction and karma is misused to legalize evil behavior. Another "funny" thing is the idea that if everything is one and differentiation is delusion then it doesn´t matter what you do to others, - the good and the bad experiences are just illusions too. So it seems that it doesn´t matter if you kill someone for egoistic purposes. At last in the higher degrees of secrets societies the members are initiated in such funny ideas that God does not exist, that good is equal with bad, that the end justifies the means, that there is no God but you, that there is no responsibility, no karma, no higher sense, that dull laws without love and awareness rule the world and so on. With a minimum of intelligence and a minimum of character you can question such statements and you can do your own studies. Then you will be able to tell truth from lies.

One of the greatest "jokes" is when such misled leaders prohibit all kinds of natural needs and things which bring joy and love into life. They say that these good things are "evil" and obstacles on the path. And as this is not enough they proclaim that the consequences are worst diseases like cancer etc. I have heard of one case where such a glorious leader died from cancer himself, - due to his evil soul. This is true karma.

At last — all those leaders and secret societies which do not say clearly what is waiting for the seeker have something to hide, - something evil to hide. True spiritual leaders/traditions are true to new seekers and inform them about the path and the milestones which have to be accomplished. "Funny" is also if you are a paying member over years in a secret society and no kind of progress can be seen, - you pay and pay and no one tells you about how to make progress or if you are stuck.

The evil ones often proclaim to belong to the light side, to do good things, to love mankind and God but later in the higher steps they show their real face, the dark side and seekers may wonder where all the light has been left, - no God, no love, no understanding.

In conclusion as a seeker one has to be very careful to step not in one of these endless traps. It is better to become a wire dancer than to be misled by ego and the dark side. And do not forget, - the truth can be felt by everyone with a healthy heart and mind.

Keep also good care about all kinds of "wise sayings". Prove them, think about them, question them as they are often misused for half-truths.

Keep your orientation on the divine virtues of love, wisdom, divine consciousness and power. "Teachings" which go against the all-embracing love and divine wisdom simply cannot be true.

Believe in God and believe in yourself.

## STATEMENT ABOUT THE SPEECH OF THE POPE

(in front of the German politicians in Berlin, 22.09.2011)

Original German statement of the Pope (extract):

"Wo die positivistische Vernunft sich allein als die genügende Kultur ansieht und alle anderen kulturellen Realitäten in den Status einer Subkultur verbanne, da verkleinert sie den Menschen, ja sie bedroht seine Menschlichkeit".

Zugleich würden extremistische und radikale Strömungen herausgefordert.

„Die sich exklusiv gebende positivistische Vernunft, die über das Funktionieren hinaus nichts wahrnehmen kann, gleicht den Betonbauten ohne Fenster, in denen wir uns Klima und Licht selber geben, beides nicht mehr aus der weiten Welt Gottes beziehen wollen", sagte der Gast.

Dabei sei nicht zu verbergen, „dass wir in dieser selbstgemachten Welt im Stillen doch aus den Vorräten Gottes schöpfen, die wir zu unseren Produkten umgestalten. Die Fenster müssen wieder aufgerissen werden, wir müssen wieder die Weite der Welt, den Himmel und die Erde sehen und all dies recht zu gebrauchen lernen", mahnte der Papst.


My translation:

„Where the positivistic reason perceives itself alone as the sufficient culture and banishes all other cultural realities in the status of a subculture, there it reduces the human being, indeed it threatened his humanity.

13

Same time, extremist and radical movements were challenged.

The wanting to appear exclusive positivistic reason, which is unable to perceive nothing beyond pure function, is similar to concrete buildings with no windows, where we supply each other with artificial self-made air and light, both are no longer from the wide world of God," the guest (pope) said.

It should not be hidden, that we draw in this self-made world in silence from the inventories of God that we transform into our (artificial) products. The windows have to be torn up again, we must again see the vastness of the world, the sky and the earth and learn all how to use them in the right, lawful way. ", warned the pope.

Statement:

(I hope my translation of the extract is understandable. The Pope makes complex sentences which are not easy to translate.)

The whole event together with the content of his speech is very interesting. For the first time a Pope visited the German Federal Parliament and also for the first time a Pope took a speech in front of (German) politicians. Additionally about eighty politicians were absent as a sign of protest. Then the Pope spoke about justice, altruism, responsibility, truth, etc. And he spoke about the positivistic reason and concrete buildings.

For an outsider this happening might be nice or a little bit strange but for an insider, an initiate it is very clear what really happened. I want to explain it here in a little bit simplified way as details are too complex.

In history there were different philosophers who represented the dark side, the Asuras. In short they proclaimed to believe only in rationality, - into the "objective" human intellect, into science, in materialism (the things you can see and measure), that no God, no spiritual beings exist, that all religions have to be destroyed, that all human beings are equal and only "good" for work and exploitation, that the "better" humans are the only existing gods and that their duty is to form their own order from the existing chaos. Indeed those philosophers were the fathers of communism and all other evil ideologies, - people as slaves to serve the gods. So one of these philosophers has invented "positivism". This is something which the "elite" still believes in although it is nonsense. For the Asuras, dark ones or simply assholes the Pope is like pure poison, - like the devil for the church, total opposites. The Asuras are represented today in all positions of power and ideology and so in most secret societies. So no wonder that obviously the whole German Federal Parliament is taken by Asuras, dark ones. Now these Asuras think that they are the enlightened ones and all religions and their leaders are "stupid", unilluminated. So you can understand why many, - so many politicians have left the speech of the Pope – it was simply pure hate, the hate between light and darkness as light means the death for darkness and dark ones and vice versa. I as a German must say that we have extraordinary assholes in our Parliament. I guess that we in Germany produce assholes in worldwide best quality. It is astonishing. But this just by the way.

So, the Pope knew before that he would enter the center of darkness and that they extremely hate him. Although he knew he took the speech in front of the vermin, the servants of darkness. And what has he done? He burned them with his intellectual brilliance and told them indirectly his opinion about them and their satanic ideas. For this he receives standing ovations from me. Very well done! So what did he say? He told them to remember of

15

justice, altruism, higher sense of life, spirituality, responsibility and so on. And then he said the main point, - that these dark ones dream of creating their own world like little gods which they are not; that they have created concrete buildings which work like ugly prisons with own artificial light and climate which makes ill and that it is time to break down this artificial bullshit to inhale the air of nature and the sunlight again, to live a healthy and lawful life with love and compassion. He used this "concrete building" in best figurative way, - very intelligent. A great fun for me was to read that many politicians were too dull to understand what the Pope talked about. I must still laugh when I think about this. These dark, total idiots which think that they are gods with the necessity to force people to suffer under their ideologies.

Have I mentioned that I do not really like these Asuras? For a period of time they might appear funny but one day they make you become fed up completely. They have become so funny and painful dull that they proclaim their insane ideas in public. Indeed it is a direct request to get into a lunatic asylum for treatment (if possible). German politicians tell a shit which is simply unbelievable. They proclaim that white is black and evil is good, that destructive, satanic behavior is necessary... The answers will come, - pure violence, rage and destruction.

A last word on the Pope respectively on the Catholic Church. Certainly there are points which one can or should see critically but most important is that the Pope is a follower of Jesus and his teachings. So although there might be darkness there is also light, more light than darkness in the Catholic Church. As far as I know the former Pope was initiated by the Rosecrucians (real ones of the East) and Benedikt follows the old Pope. Pope Paul was threatened by dark ones in his own organization. Many secret wars are going on under the surface. And today Benedikt has still a connection to Paul and receives his guidance from the astral zone.

All in all we have to support the light in all people and all religions to work successfully for the victory!

May the divine spirit enlighten all of us so that we are able to differentiate light from darkness!

The judgment of God is without any mercy. It is perfect. The punishment will be terrible. Those who believe that they are gods and kings today will be nothing more than a piece of shit tomorrow. Remember what Jesus, the great Quabbalist, has predicted.

The will of God is done upon earth.

And the vermin must vanish.

## THE BULLWHIP OF MAMMON

What has the biggest influence on life? Love, culture, religion? No, it is Mammon or the human desire for money. The whole topic is quite interesting and so I want to show here some main points.

Once upon a time people simply exchanged their services and products and the world was perfect. Then the complexity of economy increased and money as a medium for exchange was invented. Money had real value in these times as it was made of gold, silver and copper. Already in these times people started the desire to gather money, - just to have it, to have much of it, to be rich, mighty and with influence on society. So money has lost quite early its original purpose as a substitute for products and services. Money became "egocentric". Through all times people loved to steal, to maraud property from others as it is easier to ransack than to produce wealth by yourself. With the invention of money this criminal preference increased. Money is simply easier to steal than property.

(The following is a little bit simplified and exaggerated.) So thanks to robbery, evil business and political redistribution of money from the poor to the rich (leaders) the former balance of economics turned into major imbalances where a few rich men had much of everything in opposite to masses of poor which only had the right to serve the rich. Between rich and poor several middle classes with own functions grew.

Not much has changed since these early days. Still a very few people have most of the property and money of the world and the majority are normal working people or quite poor ones with a minimum to live from.

When you observe society, culture, politics, science, etc. then you can see that every topic is directly connected with money. The main questions are always "What can I earn? How much profit will I make? How much does it cost? How can we make much money with this invention, with this discovery, with these news?" Scientists work for money, culture serves money, politicians serve for money, society is constructed to serve money, - there is nothing without the idea of making money. Mammon is the one and only ideal and everything has to orientate itself on Mammon. An all-embracing perversion has taken place. When you compare the professions from former times with their image of today you can sense this. Some examples: In the past the elite, the leaders, politicians of societies felt deeply honored to serve their people. They did it not for money. Scientists have worked for the ideal of science, to discover the secrets of nature, - not for money. Everyone needs money or better said something to keep alive but money was never the one and only ideal. It was something necessary but also secondary. Human ideals were on first place. Today scientists work for big companies on the search for making money with discoveries. Politicians change their opinions quickly if you pay enough.

And which kinds of ideals do you get preached by society, by their leaders? Human ideals, divine ideals? Certainly not, - the ideals of Mammon! "Work hard, work much, let your children be indoctrinated by us, become a part of the system, don't think more than necessary, take pills if you feel bad, your ideal is to become the perfect worker, the perfect machine, our scientists (high priests) have proved that you are just a material machine with the illusion of mind and soul, your life has no other sense than to work, make career, career is your ideal, increase your consumption, consumption is the only thing which makes you happy, pay high taxes, follow your orders, we are all equal, and so on." Today everywhere the evil is implanted. For example go to a doctor, tell him that you feel ill. The doctor gives you some pills to fight the symptoms and sends you home. He does not ask about the reasons, he does not differentiate between mind, soul and physical body. He does not speak about the risks of the pills. He has no time and he gets not enough money. He is educated by the pharmaceutical industry which earns money by selling pills to ill people, - not to healthy people. Or the journalist, - he is not allowed to write what he thinks is the truth or which is important. He has to write what his boss tells him to for reasons of money, power, influence, control.

In fact humans are very busy in their life to cheat each other to earn money and the real ideals are lost. So much cheating and evil intentions cannot lead to a good life, not to health and not to happiness. The result is what we can sense everywhere today, - a world on its knees, a disaster in all aspects of human society.

The highest point of this evil system was the idea to produce paper money without real countervalue and without the control of the single states. How is it possible that all states of the world are in heavy debts? Who can give a credit to a state? A private person? A private bank? And why can be credits created from nearly nothing, from no real countervalue? This and the evil idea of the compound interest led to the necessity of forcing economics to unlimited growth. In nature there is no unlimited growth but companies have to increase their gains to be able to pay their credits. The compound interest is the bullwhip of Mammon. We all feel this bullwhip every day, - faster, higher, better! We "must" work faster. We "must" increase efficiency. Mammon says "we must" and means the workers, not the elite which collects the money. In Germany politicians have already said "we must work until the age of 79". Then "we" can die directly after work. Why do they say this? Just because there is no money for the pensions.

In conclusion we all suffer from this ideology of Mammon and his bullwhip. Mammon leads only to misery, destruction, death, - to nothing good. We need to remember the old and true human ideals, the ideals of society. Mammon has to vanish like all illusions. We have to serve the sense again. Life without sense is senseless, nonsense.

We must end the tyranny of Mammon. It is time.

No more slavery!

Statement by A.: "I think the strongest desire is the desire for love, not money."

Add: You are certainly right. Unfortunately is not love the ruling force but money. Money itself is just a form of energy but it is misused today for evil purposes. As long as we are enslaved by our financial system we have to suffer. The negative understanding of money has to be transformed into its positive opposite, - in a useful nourishing energy for all people.


## THE HERMETIC STUDY CIRCLE

On the hermetic path, especially on the path of Bardon many lone fighters are on their way. In fact there is no other possibility for spiritual development than to make it on your own. On the other hand lone fighters can join in study groups for exchange of understanding theory and real experiences from practice.

Regarding study groups an agglomeration of problems occurs, especially with the topic "magic". When you examine the open study groups in the internet then you can find always people with big egos, negative people, insane ones, pseudo gurus and unprepared ones. Certainly some innocent and good ones are among these groups. Such a mixture of different intentions, attitudes and access cannot lead to any good. In main it leads to misunderstandings, dangers and a waste of precious time.

For some more or less useful small talk such study groups might be nice but if you want to take part in a well working study group you have to regard some points.

1. First of all there have to be created clear aims for the group activity and requirements for new members. Aims are for example to support each other as brother and sisters on the path, to serve the all-embracing love and divine wisdom, and to be an ideal for others in behavior and projects. For every member a true spiritual attitude with best spiritual intentions are required. Everyone must serve the highest human ideals and everyone has to work on the refinement of his personality. Before entering the study circle the new member must dedicate himself to the four main virtues of God. He must subordinate himself to these divine virtues. The ego has to orientate itself on God.

Clear aims and the requirements for membership are the basis for this study circle. They guarantee success.

2. The law of silence has to be kept. The circle can be visible for potential members for example in the internet but its content has to be closed. This is also valid for the identity of the members.

3. Thanks to PC´s and internet it is possible to build a good structure for the studies. A first part is the apportionment of the training exercises and steps. A second structure is the theory part and the third part is built by topics which complement Bardon´s teachings. Then should be differentiated between discussions of topics, sharing of knowledge and sharing of experiences. So in conclusion for each topic in the three categories you can start discussions, share knowledge and experiences. These activities should have a scientific character. In most groups too much verbal rubbish is posted. This is not useful.

4. It is recommendable to elect a moderator who organizes all activities and keeps the lawful function upright. In main he has to manage the administration. He is not the leader but the mediator and organizer. The circle is led by a council of all members. The

members with the highest degree of spiritual maturity should have the highest weight in council matters. Decisions should been made after a clear differentiation of pro and contra on an objective basis. The council is democratic and every member has to take responsibility for his voting. For situations which require a fast action a leader should be elected who has the right to give commands until the situation is over. This can happen for security reasons or in cases of emergency.

5. Then it is necessary that every member takes part in the circle activities regularly. A weekly feedback about his spiritual studies and training should be a basis, - also a basis for discussions, help, new ideas and so on.

6. Due to the cooperation in the circle knowledge, methods and useful documents can be gathered and optimized. For example the soul mirror work with useful charts or things for training of special abilities.

7. Combined meditations and prayers are certainly also a good possibility to support each other. Here the effect of Abisheka and Satsang helps the younger ones to understand and to practice successfully.

So these were the main points for successful study circles. To include an advanced student or a master is recommendable but in reality hard to find. Students with high aims will master all steps also without any direct master.

Certainly there are also other points which have to be regarded. How should one find the fitting members? How can you be sure that all are real? And so on. From my experiences I can say that a big problem is that most people in any kind of group are up to 99% passive. No action takes place and all are waiting for the group admin to start some activity. So in conclusion the realization of such a study circle can be quite hard. But at last with the right prayers and according to the law of analogy one will find others with the same ideals. And then a real study circle will manifest itself.

## A DYNAMIC MEDITATION TECHNIQUE

There are many different forms of meditation serving special aims. In the magical and mystical training we have often the aim to manifest special characteristics and new abilities. For this purpose you can use a dynamic form of meditation which is originally used for reaching ecstasy, - unity with God. The main point here is to start with an idea and to feed this idea by dynamic repetition as long as the idea has realized from Akasha down to the mental, astral and maybe physical plane. In fact you charge the idea, make it bigger and stronger until it realizes. The more mental and emotional energy you pump into the idea the faster it manifests.

The Yoga tradition for example uses such techniques in Mantra Yoga where a single sentence is repeated endlessly. But as explained above normal repetition is just a basis but not the crown of techniques. When you repeat "The Father and I are one." and you do it with great emotions, belief and joy then you can receive an ecstatic enlightenment. It certainly depends also on your maturity, etc. but by such a simple technique great things are possible. Indeed all religions use such techniques in form of prayers and holy rituals.

For our magical or mystical purposes we just have to choose a fitting idea respectively sentence and or symbol. Imagine you want to master vital energy, an exercise of the first or second step of Bardon´s system. A fitting sentence would be "I have mastered vital energy perfectly!" or "Vital energy follows my will – always!" Now you get into your asana and repeat this sentence "endlessly" during your meditation time. Put in every sentence as much energy, will, emotions, belief, etc. as possible. Feel the joy that you have mastered vital energy. You can also mix sentences respectively add them. Important is that you strengthen the idea behind the sentences – total mastership over vital energy with all consequences! Count your repetitions with your beads. Do this meditation daily. You will experience how your reality changes to the wished for reality. You become step by step a master of vital energy.

This technique you can use for all qualities, virtues, powers, abilities, also for wishes of all kinds. It is just magic.

## THE MAGIC OF MAKING PLANS

Life is full of magic. A very interesting and unaware application of magic can be found in making plans. Everyone makes plans nearly every day. So you might ask where the magic is hidden. It is very simple but at the same time ingenious.

Imagine someone who does not make plans. He undergoes different situations of life where he reacts on the present circumstances. Such a way of life is not aim-oriented. (This is not a valuation.)

Now imagine someone who has clear visions in mind and who makes plans to realize his visions. It is an active, aim-orientated way of life. So what exactly happens here? At first you have an idea in mind, for example for creating an own business. This idea inspires your enthusiasm and so the idea grows to a bright vision backed up with a lot of positive emotions. This great amount of energy pushes you towards actions to realize your vision. Here in this example you collect all necessary information for a business plan. You inform yourself about the costs of business, the needed income, how many customers you have to serve per months and so on. For your business plan you make an analysis of profit and liquidity over three years. There you estimate fix costs, sales and more factors. Indeed you plan your future for three years. One day you are ready to start your business and then you orientate all your actions on the business plan you have created before. This business plan pushes you to reach the estimated figures. If you do not reach them then you have to adapt your whole analysis of profit. All in all you realize step by step your plans and at last your vision.

Second example: The same is true for any kind of training, - for us the training of magic. You have the vision of yourself as a master of magic, as someone who has mastered the ten steps of Bardon´s first book. You feel great enthusiasm and you make concrete plans how you will realize this. You know that there are ten steps divided into three parts with several single exercises respectively abilities, virtues or powers. So all steps with their subordinated aims can be seen as milestones on the way to mastership, - your final aim and vision. Now you can plan time and effort to reach the single aims and milestones. For example you say that you will do training every day for one hour and that you set a time frame of three months for each exercise. The three different kinds of exercises you do in a parallel way, - physical training as fitness training, mental and astral training in the meditation hour in the evening. Now you make an

Excel list with the training steps and exercises and the estimated time for full success together with the calendar dates. Now you can see that you will have mastered clairvoyance at Friday, the 28th of September in 2015, - for example. You have planned your future with all single steps and aims. Now you can start to work according to your plans to manifest your aims. The settings of your plans will have a clear and strong influence on you to fulfill them.

In conclusion: Equal to the kind of plans and visions you have it is always the same magical thing. What do you do when you set aims, concrete, well defined aims for your future? You set actively and consciously new and positive seeds of karma, new causes for effects, consequences for your life and future. This is the secret, the magic. Ask yourself: How should something realize which was never envisioned, which was never defined, never planted? It simply cannot realize. A farmer cannot reap fruits when he has never planted seeds on his field. Clear? So in fact we have to plant consciously the wished for seeds of karma to reap one day in the future the envisioned fruits. When you only react in a not aim-oriented way of life then you depend on the grace of fate. But as a master you manifest actively what you wish for.

And here the secret of magic unveils. You can only manifest what you have envisioned in the finished state because the idea of this wished for, finished state has to grow and to realize. Only this idea can manifest all necessary circumstances for its appearance. This might feel strange or wrong for humans but it is a metaphysical fact taught by all spiritual masters. Everyone can experience the truth of this. By the way the finished, perfect state of something wished for (e. g. you as a master magician) in the presence is a matter of its Akasha nature, - the world of ideas as Platon already stated. And as Bardon said – humans draw the ideas of the Akasha plane and manifest them down through all three planes.

Maybe you do not really believe in estimation. But this is absolutely unimportant. Important is only to plant the seeds of your wished for karma and to believe in your vision. Then the rest will manifest in form of analogue situations which help you to realize your aims.

Certainly things have to be realistic. Realization has something to do with being realistic.

So make plans, perform magic and become the master of your life.

## ENHANCED TECHNIQUE FOR AUTOSUGGESTION

I have presented already a special technique for autosuggestion. The main point of this technique was to set yourself into the sphere of your subconsciousness and to do autosuggestion directly there. You can enhance this technique further on: Set yourself, your awareness into the center of your subconsciousness which you think of like a big sphere similar to the exercises of Bardon. Now charge this sphere also with Akasha. Then do your autosuggestion. Additionally you can use software like Neuro-Programmer which provides special sounds for deep states of consciousness and possibilities to record your autosuggestion together with the sounds. In conclusion: This is the easiest and most effective way of self-influence, affirmation and autosuggestion.

## MAGICAL INVESTMENTS

Imagine that you have four accounts, each one with a special purpose. Regularly you pay in and take of money at each account to finance the foreseen purposes. Maybe you have an account for holidays, maybe another one for sports, one for family, etc. To use this technique of four accounts instead of one for everything has some advantages. For example you have always the overview how much money (energy) you can place for the disposal of one purpose. Also you do not forget to pay in for each one. So indeed all your purposes is served well. This means that you have good holidays because you save money for this, you have enough money for your family, enough for sports and so on. In different words you make investments for all these aspects of your life.

Now imagine that you use this technique for magical investments. For example you can invest energy regularly for success, health, protection, happiness, happy family, also the development of abilities and qualities, etc. You just have to choose what you wish for, then you put it into a sentence, maybe you anchor it with a fitting symbol and then you charge it daily. Let´s take an example – success. Your sentence could be "I am successful!" or "I am a winner!" A fitting symbol is the raised winner fist or another sign of success, winning, power. Now you can charge this idea with repeating the sentence, will and fitting emotions, also with prayers and meditation. The result is that you have built a battery which becomes stronger by daily charging. This battery is automatically connected with you and every time you need some success energy then you receive it for having success. With the passing time the battery will have such a big influence on you that your personality (structure) changes and success becomes a part of your nature.

This works for all kinds of purposes. Just invest energy for your wishes regularly and you will gain the fruits.

29

## Saturation and Perfection

Today I want to share some thoughts about one of the main principles behind life, the principle which keeps us and all other creatures busy, in action. It is the desire for saturation, for perfection or in different words for completeness and total balance.

When I think back to my time at school then I remember where our teacher for chemistry explained us the nature of the different elements of the periodic table. He said that the difference is just in the amount of the positrons, neutrons and electrons. So when you change these parts then you have a different element with different qualities. The teacher explained further on that all elements "long" for perfection, the state of the gold atom which is complete and perfect in its composition. It is in perfect balance regarding structure and the amount of positrons, neutrons and electrons. And because of its perfection gold has no "desire" to join chemical reactions with other elements. Back then these insights into the nature of the material elements were fascinating for me. If someone was able to change the amount of the parts of an element he could transform all elements into any element. And further on all elements "try" to reach completeness, perfection by joining chemical reactions. Very interesting.

This desire for completeness, saturation and balance can be found everywhere. Nothing exists which does not long for this perfection. The divine being is in this static state which appears as Akasha, the Eternal Light or the sphere of light which is "behind" the sphere of the sun. But God is not created. God is beyond creation. Creation and creatures are in a dynamic state of balancing. Everything originates from the balanced, static state and everything wants to come back to this state. We can call this evolution. In this evolution everything and everyone tries to reach a certain kind of balance by joining other elements of creation. Step by step everything reaches higher levels of balance, of saturation and completeness. Highest fulfillment is gained by spiritual enlightenment, by the unity with God, the primal source of life.

Everything we humans do we do it to satisfy our needs, to balance the imbalance we are in. Creation is based on this dynamic form of imbalance and balancing activities. So we have to look for food, we have to sleep, to work, to find friends, someone to love, etc. This all repeats from incarnation to incarnation. But also from incarnation to incarnation we refine ourselves and come closer to the divine origin, to the state of perfection.

While normal people have to look for balance in the outer world, spiritual people receive balance directly from the divine source. Figuratively speaking when normal people satisfy their need of love with a glass of love, spiritual people do not need a glass as they bath in an unlimited ocean of love (of best quality). These are the differences. Indeed spiritual people are saturated with love. They are balanced in this and other aspects. This means also completeness as nothing is missing and it means perfection. When you are saturated, satisfied then you are independent from desires, you are free and you have a free choice. You are like gold. You are superior, sovereign.

And indeed the whole magical and later mystical training with all kinds of energy leads to saturation in all aspects of mind and soul. You simply have enough of all elements and virtues. You are complete. And now you are free to decide which chemical reactions you want to join. You can define the circumstances of your life. You can say yes or no. You can take part or leave. It is your free decision. (From a higher point of view this is valid but during incarnations there are certainly factors like divine tasks and missions, divine will and divine plans which you follow with your free decision to do so. But there is no force behind it, just wisdom, insight and love.)

In conclusion it is a major aim of life, of humans and all other creatures to reach a state of saturation, of peace, balance, completeness, perfection and fullness. With this state the interest in new incarnations decreases or vanishes. Several further points about this topic could be mentioned but I leave it up to the reader to meditate about it.

## QUESTION ABOUT A SIMPLE WAY TO LEARN MAGIC

I read this in William Mistele's website.

Questions and Answers

Question: Is there a simple way to learn magic without having to do all the occult exercises?

Answer. Yes. You take three minutes to three hours each day of your life. With this time, you imagine you are different things. The order does not really matter. What matters is that in the beginning you follow your interests and then branch out into every conceivable image.

Imagine you are other people--all kinds of people. Think of people you know, people from history, people from the future, and various ethnic and religious groups. Imagine you are every kind of animal and things from nature--trees, bugs, mountains, stones, minerals, seas, clouds, planets, stars, and so forth. Later on, imagine too that you are different spirits.

As you do this exercise, notice carefully the effect of the imagery on your mind, feelings, and body. Notice how each of your five senses is shaped and extended by the exercise. At some point in your practice, you should be able to notice that if you imagine you are a seal or another person, you can get impressions that are not a function of your imagination. Holding the image of something in your mind without distraction, you form a psychic connection. This link can be extended and developed. It turns into telepathy, clairvoyance, and clairsentience.

This exercise is part of the study of omnipresence. Under the law of love, you are free to join with anything in the universe. This is no limit on or exception to this rule. You open your mind and heart and become one with anything and everything that exists. This is a basic exercise if not the basic exercise in magic as I understand it. It is worth learning and practicing for a life time.

I think those who cannot find a steady time to meditate step by step as taught by Bardon may try this or something similar to this. What do you think of this exercise? Can something be added to it? Or how can we vary the exercise? I also think the depth point meditation (Akasha exercise) in "Initiation Into Hermetics" Step five may work as this exercise that William Mistele mentions. What do you think about this too?

Thank you.

T.

Hi T.,

Mistele is right with his answer. You can learn a part of magic this way which deals with the Akasha principle and the abilities of the consciousness. The mind is independent from time and space and so you can move your mind and melt it with everything and everyone in the universe. When you do the described exercise you train this ability and you receive all kinds of impressions with your senses. These impressions have to do with clairvoyance, telepathy and so on.

The main point is that it is just a part of magic and it does not replace the whole training. But it is a useful exercise and indeed not really different to what Bardon describes for training the mind in a later step.

The exercise or training of the mind is absolutely unlimited. An useful aspect is to melt your mind with Buddhas, enlightened masters, holy people, divine spirits, God, etc. so that you take part in the spiritual nature of them which influences yourself in best way.

Beside this all kinds of beings and objects are useful for this exercise.

Maybe one useful hint: This exercise has a main focus on "letting go". This means you start as yourself but then you let go and shift to the other being and this is a matter of time and imagination. So you imagine that you are for example Buddha Amitabha in the pure land. While your imagination becomes better and more complete with the passing time your awareness of yourself vanishes and you feel like Amitabha. You take part in his nature. So this shift of mind comes naturally after a certain time because of the increasing imagination.

As always I recommend experiments and many repetitions for success.

The setting into the Akasha point is a little bit special. It means full control of the object or being for charging purposes for example.

At last - just follow Bardon´s and Mistele´s descriptions. There is nothing you can do wrong here. And it is very interesting to practice.

Ray

## Technique for Karma Yoga

As you know karma yoga deals with the balancing of your karma account, - to dissolve bad karma by doing good things in a selfless way. The accumulation of positive karma leads to liberty and enlightenment. Originally karma yoga was a part of Maha yoga, the path to spiritual perfection. Certainly every real spiritual master or magician practices Karma yoga naturally. It is pure service for creation in the name of divine love and grace.

There are endless possibilities to practice Karma yoga, to do good things. One interesting technique I want to share here:

Due to the worldwide demonstrations against the domination of the disastrous financial system I have thought about how I could give support for mankind to master these challenges. I decided myself to pray to God to bless mankind and the earth with divine love and enlightenment. The divine love I chose for clearing, healing and connecting people to God and to each other to feel like a big family. Love has great powers. Enlightenment is needed to let people understand how to solve the problems and to feel connected with God. While I pray to God for love and enlightenment I imagine the earth with mankind and all its creatures in an all-permeating energy of pink color according to the cosmic letter Y (Akasha love). I imagine that this all-embracing and all-permeating love energy dissolves all negative energies and gives healing and love to all beings. I keep this imagination for a while. Then I imagine that the earth with all beings is bathed in white spiritual enlightening power. The pink energy I keep by and the white energy I add. So enlightenment comes together with love and the prayer to God for his blessings. So much about the technique.

The point is that I normally do not like respectively perform such prayers just because a single person cannot raise so much power to clear, heal and enlighten the whole world. It is certainly a good and right intention but the aim cannot be reached this way. If you find a lot of spiritual people who would perform all the same imagination and prayer then real changes are possible.

As it is my heart's desire that people awake and positive changes manifest I have kept this prayer. As a result I have made some positive but unexpected discoveries. People who are connected to me have received the blessings of love and enlightenment and show love for me as an unconscious way of saying "thank you for these blessings". I also made some unexpected progress in healing old blockades. These are signs of karma yoga, of clearing, healing and balancing karma.

So indeed this technique is very useful for the spiritual path of karma yoga. Dissolve your blockades, clear yourself from bad karma, heal yourself, heal your relationships, draw positive influences into your life, become free, create the basis for a happy life, prepare the path for spiritual success and become a servant of God and creation.

## HUMAN WISHES VERSUS DIVINE AIMS

This topic is an interesting phenomenon. Humans dream of love, peace, a happy life, fun, prosperity, a nice house, nice surroundings, holidays, traveling and so on. During their incarnation they have to experience that often only a fraction of their wishes and dreams come true. Why do our wishes not realize the way we would appreciate it? Apart from the high degree of difficulty in the material realm the reason lies in the superior divine aims which life follows. The main aim is the spiritual evolution, the refinement process. For this reason every human being incarnates with a task to master, - a lesson to learn, something to grow from. These lessons are in parts not funny but necessary as they mean learning through the negative principle. Other tasks deal with the development of new abilities and knowledge. Simplified we can say that the lessons of life contain in most cases a negative part and a positive part. Further on derived from the main aim and regarding karma humans have to balance all the effects which manifest by their actions (of former life times). This is normally really much work.

In higher states of consciousness respectively at the end of their incarnation or later after the physical death, people become aware that everything in life was a necessary experience and that it was useful for their development. In fact life was not possible in a different way due to the personal circumstances, the personal seeds of karma.

I must admit that such insights especially for your own life are quite strange but you understand the logic behind it. When you have to suffer then such insights bring relief. It also lets you understand why you are confronted with things you do not like, which are contrary to you.

At last this explains why in main all these "think positive" techniques do not really work without restrictions. Only a real spiritual master is liberated from fate due to his long term training and refinement. And only a spiritual master can realize his wishes without interfering with the superior divine aims. But I must say that a spiritual master has brought his wishes into accordance with the divine aims and laws.

Humans have only a restricted scope for the realization of their wishes. Like Bardon says the free will has to be deserved through spiritual mastership. Until this happen humans are more or less a plaything of fate. With the increasing of personal refinement and maturity, the free will together with mastership in life is increasing too.

As a consequence of these explanations humans have to look for whishes which go together with the spiritual aims (development), which are realizable and second, they should work on the balancing of their karma to dissolve restrictions respectively blockades in life.

We all have to look for the sense in life, in everything we do as the sense is divine.

## SOME WORDS ABOUT THE NATURE OF FRANZ BARDON

From time to time there are discussions about Bardon as a person in internet forums. These discussions show that Bardon isn't really understood by many followers especially by younger ones respectively beginners. The main problem is that the readers of his books do not really think through what the explanations indirectly say about Bardon. The second problem is that most students do not have the practical experience to know which kind of transformation is reached by the magical and mystical training. And so they are not able to understand him and his personality.

Simplified said, the being which incorporated itself in the physical body of Franz Bardon was a god, a superior being, completely refined, of divine nature, a spiritual grand master. This master with the name Arion has assumed with his mental body the physical and the astral body of the original Franz Bardon while his spirit was set for a new birth under better circumstances. This explains why Arion has had to cope with the karma of the original Franz Bardon, - just because the astral body and the physical body were of the unrefined imbalanced energy and structure of the original. Arion has in fact taken over the whole life respectively karma of the original Franz Bardon. And no one is allowed to change simply the karma of another person. No master can do this for his students and also not for normal people. So it should be comprehensible that Arion could not intervene in the karma of the original Franz Bardon which was contained by his physical and astral body. Indeed it was a great sacrifice for Arion to incorporate into a normal human. Due to the karma of the original Franz Bardon, Arion had to suffer from certain diseases and problems as it is described in Frabato. The only kind of intervention for bettering his health was normal medicine which Dr. M. K. gave him and tricks like using the nicotine effects of cigarettes to increase his performance. But this is also described in Frabato.

By the way a spiritual master like Arion has absolutely no interest in being celebrated or treated like a VIP as there is no sense in it. In the same way his proclaimed incarnations are of no interest and meaning at all. These details simply play any role for what he is. Only a real master is able to write such books with all the detailed information which can only be derived from real experience. When you have made progress in the training then you can prove everything that Arion describes. Then you will also know what it means to be of divine nature and what gods are. Normal humans simply cannot understand these things as they are not able to experience them.

A last aspect of this topic: Although you are of divine nature you will have still aspects of the human nature. Depending on the spiritual maturity they can be more or less. Someone like Arion has had such aspects only at the surface and so he had to put effort in appearing as a human. When your nature is so much refined to divine standards then not much human qualities remain. This is just a fact.

By the way the Dalai Lama is also an incarnated god but he keeps this secret as far as possible and tries to act like a normal human. It is sometimes quite interesting to observe how he constructs answers to questions of interviewers to keep a human image.

Jesus was certainly also a god. Therefore he said that he is a son of God and that he and his father are one, - same nature.

In the history of mankind many gods have incarnated to teach spiritual seekers and many spiritual students have reached this degree of refinement.

## GOOD ADVICE BY ERIC IDLE

Eric Idle, the well-known member of Monty Python is a great comedian. He has written several funny songs. One famous song is "Always look on the bright side of life". This song shows the right way to manage the dark sides of life, - with laughter and this I mean seriously. When you receive bad news then you are somehow shocked and maybe paralyzed. This state you can break in best way with laughter. Singing and dancing is also useful. It is necessary to get rid of the bad state to be able to go on. Life means always to move on and dark situations will change to better. It is all a matter of passing time.

So when you feel devastated then force yourself to laughter. It will be your liberation. Then dance and sing the song of Eric Idle, - if you like:

Words and music by Eric Idle

"Always look on the bright side of life"

Some things in life are bad
They can really make you mad
Other things just make you swear and curse.
When you're chewing on life's gristle
Don't grumble, give a whistle
And this'll help things turn out for the best...

And...always look on the bright side of life...
Always look on the light side of life...

If life seems jolly rotten
There's something you've forgotten
And that's to laugh and smile and dance and sing.
When you're feeling in the dumps
Don't be silly chumps
Just purse your lips and whistle - that's the thing.

And...always look on the bright side of life...
Always look on the light side of life...

For life is quite absurd
And death's the final word
You must always face the curtain with a bow.
Forget about your sin - give the audience a grin
Enjoy it - it's your last chance anyhow.

So always look on the bright side of death
Just before you draw your terminal breath

Life's a piece of shit
When you look at it
Life's a laugh and death's a joke, it's true.
You'll see it's all a show
Keep 'em laughing as you go
Just remember that the last laugh is on you.

And always look on the bright side of life...
Always look on the right side of life...
(Come on guys, cheer up!)
Always look on the bright side of life...
Always look on the bright side of life...
(Worse things happen at sea, you know.)
Always look on the bright side of life...
(I mean - what have you got to lose?)
(You know, you come from nothing - you're going back to nothing.
What have you lost? Nothing!)
Always look on the right side of life...

# Q: WHAT CAN I DO WHEN BARDON'S TEACHINGS SEEM TO BE TOO DIFFICULT FOR PRACTICE?

Hi A.,

concerning your question there are some different aspects to regard:

1. Bardon's teachings can be seen as the description of universal milestones which everyone in a spiritual training will meet on his way. So it is not obligatory to follow exactly his training. You can take a different system to make spiritual progress and you can complete it with Bardon's teachings. For example it makes sense to look for a teacher to learn meditation, concentration and imagination. Then you can look for a system which helps you to refine yourself and to raise your awareness. Both you find for example in the Bon Buddhism which is very close to Bardon. Besides this you can learn to work with vital energy and the chakras when you take part in workshops of Pranic Healers. So in these ways you get access to higher abilities and refinement. But please know that especially the Western esoteric traditions have many traps and bad qualities. So I cannot recommend them for real development. There is too much evil hiding under the surface of many Western schools. So please orientate yourself on the Eastern schools.

2. Bardon's teachings are already very useful to study them with your intellect. It increases your knowledge in best way. So at least an intellectual study of his books is very good.

3. If you want to increase magical abilities then there is a quite simple method which is useful and good. But it cannot replace a complete training. It is from William Mistele and you can practice it as you like to:

"You take three minutes to three hours each day of your life. With this time, you imagine you are different things. The order does not really matter. What matters is that in the beginning you follow your interests and then branch out into every conceivable image. Imagine you are other people--all kinds of people. Think of people you know, people from history, people from the future, and various ethnic and religious groups. Imagine you are every kind of animal and things from nature--trees, bugs, mountains, stones, minerals, seas, clouds, planets, stars, and so forth. Later on, imagine too that you are different spirits. As you do this exercise, notice carefully the effect of the imagery on your mind, feelings, and body. Notice how each of your five senses is shaped and extended by the exercise. At some point in your practice, you should be able to notice that if you imagine you are a seal or another person, you can get impressions that are not a function of your imagination. Holding the image of something in your mind without distraction, you form a psychic connection. This link can be extended and developed. It turns into telepathy, clairvoyance, and clairsentience. This exercise is part of the study of omnipresence. Under the law of love, you are free to join with anything in the universe. This is no limit on or exception to this rule. You open your mind and heart and become one with anything and everything that exists. This is a basic exercise if not the basic exercise in magic as I understand it. It is worth learning and practicing for a life time."

4. The training of Bardon is certainly not easy. But in main it is a matter of stubborn training and a true spiritual attitude. With a real heart´s desire for spiritual development you get support from spiritual beings. But also then training takes much time.

So at last I think that many students choose little detours to reach their aims - things like Pranic Healing, Taoistic Alchemy, maybe Reiki, Buddhism techniques and so on. Look for your personal and individual fitting detour to get results and progress. You will find something good for sure. There are enough teachers available for smaller and bigger initiations.

I hope this was useful for you.

With best regards,

Ray


## HELL AND MOTHER HOLLE

In the Germanic fairy tales and religious traditions Mother Holle occurs as a friendly old woman living in heaven. She appears like a goddess with positive influences on humans and nature. Long time ago when the first Christian missionaries came to Germany and the Northern countries they demonized the old established gods and goddesses of the indigenous people. An interesting thing are here the terms Holle and hell which have further meanings in German like light and bright and also secret. The Christian missionaries turned the originally positive terms into their dark opposites, - the hell with its hellfire and the suffering souls. In contrary originally hell meant heaven, something like the Elysian Fields of the Greek. The term devil had also different origins than the Christian missionaries made of it. These things are quite fascinating when you examine the similarities of terms in language.

## BEYOND GOOD AND BAD

The topic of good and bad seems to be a never ending story. There are always people who believe that due to spiritual or magical training good and bad lose their meaning and so these people can do what they like, - here especially bad egoistic things as they have gone "beyond" this polarity. This is certainly real nonsense and a misunderstanding of spiritual teachings. There are still the laws of creation, - here the law of karma which will be always valid. So when you do something evil or destructive then you have to take responsibility for the bad fruits, - equal how refined or mighty you are. Even when you think that you can give orders for an evil action to a spirit, you have to face the consequences as you keep the responsibility. So in fact there is no escape from karma.

In fact the original teachings have a different meaning. Imagine you become a real magician with divine authority. Then you know the nature, function and work of the positive hierarchy and of the negative hierarchy. Depending on your mission or task you have the right to choose a fitting spirit, - angel or demon to accomplish the task or part of the mission. Demons serve here for lawful punishment. The negative hierarchy has its sense like the positive one. There is no discrimination.

In fact all depends on the divine laws and the actual situation with aims and needs to fulfill. No one is able to withdraw himself from the judgment of Divine Providence and the lords of karma.

So do not care about the illusions of a few trapped people.

## Experiment

Dear fellows,

I have found a small experiment which you can try if you like:

Take a flat bowl. Fill it with water. Then let a drop of oil fall into the center of the water surface. Now try to move this drop of oil.

Variations:

Charge yourself with vital energy and then try it. Alternatively charge yourself with earth element. Third - charge yourself with fire element or electric fluid and try it.

Have fun!

Ray

## Using mantras

Some time ago I have already written about the use of mantras. Today I want to give some further hints. First of all I must say that I am very familiar with Hinduism and Buddhism, - that I have a good connection to their spiritual realms. That makes it easy for me to work with their teachings. On the other hand everyone can use them for his benefit or can look for similar techniques in his own tradition.

I want to focus today on Hinduism but there are certainly similarities to Buddhism. In Hinduism we have for every psychic human center (chakra) an according god or goddess together with a holy bija mantra (sound/word) and certainly also special qualities and powers. Here we see the great analogy between macrocosm and microcosm – the gods and spiritual realms in the universe with the corresponding centers in the human body. The bija sounds are very powerful. They are related with the creative cosmic language. The bijas are not only used directly to activate and refine the analogue chakras but also as parts of "normal" mantras. In these mantras the bijas give extra power. So indeed they are more powerful than other mantras. In general with the recitation and repetition of mantras you connect yourself to the analogue god or goddess and you receive his/her blessings and support. The gods have always special characteristics and powers and so they provide only specific blessings and powers to the mantra user. This must be regarded.

Let´s come now to the technique: First of all you think about your needs and wishes and list them up. Then you make a research for the gods of Hinduism like Vishnu, Shiva, Brahma, Lakshmi, Durga, Saraswati and so on. Look for their characteristics and powers, also for their mantras and for which purpose they are used. You will find such details also in good books. Now gather the fitting mantras with the analogue gods according to your needs and wishes. Look for nice pictures or statues of the gods. The pictures you can print or you can buy them in online shops. Choose a nice place in at home where you can put the pictures or statues. Add the mantras and your wishes to them. If you like you can treat the pictures and statues with fluid condensers like Bardon describes it. You can repeat the mantras in front of the pictures and statues of the gods as required to receive their blessings and support. I recommend to do this with a loving, receptive and thankful attitude for a few minutes to half an hour. While you repeat the mantra you look at the god or goddess to build up a deeper connection. Imagine that you can communicate with the god. Tell him what you wish for. Tell him about your needs. Ask him to help you and to bless you. And certainly thank him cordially for his support. Believe and feel that you receive his blessings. Put also some nice flowers in front of the pictures and statues. This is a nice gesture. Indeed it is all somehow already a kind of altar. You can use the mantras for yourself, your family and job, also for your spiritual development.

Let´s take a few examples:

1.  Om Krishna guru
    This mantra is a recommendation of Swami Sivananda Radha. The god is Krishna and the purpose is to increase your divine guidance. Krishna is a form/incarnation of Vishnu and with this very familiar with Akasha. So by repetition of this mantra you increase your receptiveness for divine guidance.
2.  Om hrim dum Durgayai namah
    This is a call to Durga. She blesses you with protection and she destroys bad influences. This can be quite useful. Here we have altogether three bijas – Om, Hrim and Dum.
3.  Govinda jai jai
    This mantra awakes and increases divine love with the help of Krishna.
4.  Om shrim maha Lakshmyai svaha
    The goddess Lakshmi is called to bless you with wealth on all three planes, good business and fulfillment of wishes.

So as you can see all aspects of life can be covered with the gods and goddesses of Hinduism, - remember that there are gods for all chakras and with this for all human aspects. Additionally there are always several mantras for one god to cover the different qualities and powers of him. So it is recommendable to choose the right mantras for all your needs, - all matters of your life and to repeat them frequently to have a happy and blessed life. If you do not exactly know how the mantras are spoken then please take a look at youtube. There you can find probably all mantras.

At last a special technique: You can speak the mantras by using your imagination. For example you can imagine a room or your flat or your office where you speak the mantra into its center to fill the whole space. This is indeed a kind of blessing technique. Then you can also imagine yourself as a sphere (microcosm) where you speak in the same way the mantra into its center (your center/Akasha point) to fill your whole microcosm with it. These techniques which use the Akasha principle are quite powerful with good influences on you respectively the space/room.

The use of mantras is certainly somehow like praying and we find prayers or mantras in all religious traditions. This form of communication and worshipping of the spiritual realms has its own beauty and does much good for the soul. Imagine you have prayed to God or gods for a certain topic respectively you have repeated mantras then you have a better feeling for this matter. You know that you receive blessings and support to master your challenge or you know that you take part in the divine cornucopia for example. These are good feelings.

Experiment:

Try separately the repetition of these mantras for 10 to 30 minutes and observe what you experience on all three planes. Speak the mantras into your whole microcosm. Please regard that they have to be pronounced in the Indian way, - not English.

Mantras:

1.    Mantras for the chakras: Lam, Vam, Ram, Yam, Ham, Om

2.  Mantras of the gods and goddesses: Aim, Dum, Gam, Ham, Hrim, Klim, Krim, Kshraum, Shrim

When you make good experiences then look them up and deepen your understanding about these mantras. They are indeed quite useful.


## HYPNOSIS AND PARAPSYCHOLOGY

It is a common phenomenon that old beliefs and old knowledge is clothed into new dresses. Many aspects of religion and magic have been renamed and integrated into science and healing treatments. In their new clothes they appear "normal", innocent, free from strange connotations but certainly they work as ever. Autosuggestion and hypnosis are good examples. Especially hypnosis was in former days just a magical ability to work in many ways with the so called occult, - the hidden aspects of man and creation. Parts of the occult aspects of humans are a field for research in psychology. Several exercises of Bardon – magic, yoga, Buddhism and so on you can find there as techniques of psychotherapy. Quite funny to discover. Then there is a field of research which is called parapsychology which just means that this field is beyond normal psychology. Especially here you can find all kinds of occult topics like clairvoyance, working with pendulum and Ouija boards. All kinds of supernatural abilities are tested and developed. This happens under the guise of science. The term science has already become especially here an empty shell as there are countless "theories", better said opinions and models about these topics. This is also true for normal psychology. The problem here is simply that the materialistic philosophy is not able to explain reality. But all this just by the way. The main point is that everyone can take seminars today (further education) in hypnosis and also in hypnotic parapsychology with the full range of occult experiments. This includes in fact magical abilities like clairvoyance, telepathy, communication with beings on higher realms, levitation, materialization and dematerialization and so on. With special hypnotic abilities you can do research in these fields. And certainly you can train your own abilities. I know one provider in Germany where you can learn these things with a scientific approach and far away from "magic". From my point of view this is much better than to join any "magical group". Such providers are probably in all countries available. So if you want to learn hypnosis for yourself and for the positive use to treat others and if you want to use it for magic then have a look for a good provider of hypnosis and parapsychology in your country.

## SENSING ANIMALS

You can use your magical skills for a deeper sensing of other beings, of humans, animals and beings of higher nature. This can be quite interesting. Some time ago I was on a market where birds of prey have been shown. I am not often face to face with a big eagle and so I have taken a closer look. In this moment I have sensed his special nature. The eagle was of pure electric air element like you find it in the greater heights and also in the cosmic letter A. This was fascinating to discover. With this very powerful air element I have sensed further qualities of the eagle like perfect clarity, sharpness and speed. So the eagle is indeed the master of the air, - of the air element. When you shift your consciousness, your sense into an eagle you will experience these things by yourself. Other birds appear in a different way. For example sparrows are of the normal air element. Their qualities are analogue to it. They love to fly back and forth. They sing and talk very much. These are all attributes of the normal air element. Sparrows live in normal heights so that they are not really influenced by the strong electric air element like eagles. When you sense butterflies then you can experience that they are also beings of the air element but they embody finer qualities like lightness, airy joy and inner peace. They have analogies with the heart chakra. They are fine and beautiful beings.

Then I have also sensed lions, tigers and cheetahs. Lions have a very interesting quality of the sun sphere. It is the quality of being an unchallenged king. The point is that the lions know that they are kings in their territory and that the other animals know that too. So indeed there is no necessity for them to show it. It is like having a VIP-Pass with full access. You only have to show it and you get everything you want. So lions have a natural and absolute self-esteem, self-confidence - "Move along, here comes the king!". Due to this they do not mind to sleep and laze over the day in "public" in their territory. Different to the lions are the tigers. From a human point of view they have certainly the same status like lions but their nature is quite different. Tigers are real "power packs". They seem to have unlimited power, are very active and agile. Their quality of power is absolute and unchallenged. They do not use a VIP-Pass. The absolute self-confidence of a lion and the absolute power of a tiger are qualities which are developed in the magical training and which you need to show your authority and might in magical operations. The sharpness and clarity of an eagle belongs certainly also to the magical unity with God. I find it quite fascinating to sense divine qualities in the animal realm. I certainly must add that these qualities of eagle, lion and tiger are a matter of their energetic nature and driven by instinct as higher intelligence and self-awareness are missing. Ego and a good degree of intelligence can be sensed at chimpanzees. They have self-awareness. They have an ego (in a neutral meaning) and they have needs, desires and wishes. So they are quite busy every day to satisfy their "egoistic" needs. Therefor the social interaction in their groups is very active.

Interesting is also to observe the animals of the water realms. The water element has the strongest influence on aquatic animals in comparison to the other elements and their realms and animals. For example land animals are influenced by all four elements and so they are quite free respectively do not suffer when one element is stronger. But fish are very dependent on the water (element) which they live in. Normal fish has therefore a pure water element nature. Dolphins for example are different. They embody also the water element but they have a refined nature which expressed the watery joy of life combined with a nice form of intelligence. Big whales have qualities of space, somehow of endless space similar to Akasha with further watery aspects. The water realms with its water element are connected to the sphere of Venus and Neptune. So their qualities are reflected in the water world. There can be found so much beauty and fineness under water, also a form of higher unity.

These are just a few examples of the great diversity of the animal realm. It is up to you to discover further secrets. Maybe I have inspired you for own research.

## SHIFTING ON THE META LEVEL

The mind is somehow fixed in soul and body. Due to this the perception of oneself, others and the environment we live in, is filtered by one´s own personality. So what we perceive, think and feel depends on the individual and relative personal point of view. This is certainly quite natural and normal. It is also okay but this subjective perception of the world provides many problems. Let´s take one common example. You and another person are in a conflict. You speak from your point of view and the other person from his point of view. The argumentation gets more and more intensive but no progress in the matter takes place. The situation is stuck. The problem is that both of you are fixed in the personal perception of the situation. Now you have the possibility to shift your mind and perception on a higher, objective level, - the Meta level which is beyond the two personalities. The Meta level can also be called third-person perspective or divine/higher point of view. You can also imagine that you are an alien which observes the situation. These different names depend on the actual situation. Important is to change the perspective to a higher point of view for a better understanding, for clarity and for finding a fitting solution. In the example you shift your perception and your thinking on the Meta level and from there you understand both of you and the situation. It is a holistic understanding which is not limited by personality. The use of the Meta level technique brings many benefits for all aspects of life. A spiritual master is trained in perceiving the world from a higher point of view. So he has a superior understanding of everything. The Meta level is certainly super-personal, - in best case divine. A spiritual master has developed this super-personal mind/perception with the development of his crown chakra, - his divine center, his divine consciousness. Already as a student of magic you are asked to take this position to observe the way you think, feel and behave. So indeed it is very useful to go on distance to yourself, to your personality and to question your perception, your thoughts, emotions and behavior. Beside this it can be very useful to withdraw your mind onto the Meta level when you are confronted with negative people. So you do not take aggression or bad behavior personally. You know that it is the problem of the other persons, - not your own. The more you grow the more you relax from the bad behavior in the world. And one day you reach the degree of mastership like all true spiritual masters and masters of martial arts where you are centered in your Self. It is the mastership of tension and relaxation. In this way you have also mastered fears and stress. A higher point of view provides indeed real relief.

## THE PROCESS OF MASTERING NEW ABILITIES IN MAGIC

The exercises of Bardon appear often like something of a different planet, - far away from our normal life and comprehension. "How should I ever be able to do this?" you might think. Then you start training such a strange exercise and nothing happens. You are frustrated. Maybe you get real doubts about mastering the training at all or about Bardon or yourself. Maybe you think that one has to be superhumanly talented to make it. These are quite common experiences of a lot of interested seekers.

These are certainly the results of a "first contact" with Bardon and his training system. But these are not the final results. For success in Bardon´s training you should know and understand a lot. One point is in fact that the whole training is very demanding in time, effort and personal requirements like strong will, devotion, patience, right attitude and belief. On the other hand success is built on pure, excessive and regular training over months and years. Training leads always and everywhere to results.

Beside the personal requirements which you have to bring with you, it is useful to understand how a new ability manifests itself by training. When you comprehend the steps of manifestation then the training becomes easier or better to accomplish for you. In the following I try to explain these steps to you.

In step zero you and the new ability have nothing in common like to different worlds knowing nothing from each other. This is especially true for magic as unknown realms of existence are touched and unknown parts of the own personality have to be developed. Magic with all its topics is obviously the strangest thing on earth. The problem is that you have no experiences with other similar things which you could use as a good basis for starting the work. For example if you want to start with martial arts then you have seen already martial artists in training and you know other forms of physical training. This makes it easier for you to start it as you can integrate a new topic into already existing experiences. This is in magic nearly impossible. And this is one of the biggest problems. Learning becomes difficult due to these circumstances.

So in the first step you have to become familiar with the exercise, with the ability, with the whole new topic. You have to penetrate it mentally; you have to comprehend all aspects of it. This is possible by meditation and much research concerning Bardon´s books and explanations and also other spiritual teachings. Many exercises are well known and practiced in other spiritual traditions and religions like Yoga, Buddhism and so on. Thanks to your comprehensive studies and meditations you are able to assimilate the topic mentally, - intellectually. This is indeed a first useful and necessary step. It is in fact a form of Eucharist like Bardon means it, - incorporation/assimilation.

In a second step you have to prepare yourself mentally and emotionally on the training to gain the new ability. This includes the planning of your training and the forming of a positive attitude, - an expectation of full success together with the will, devotion and belief for full success. You really must experience yourself with the new ability, with having success in your imagination. Know the success, feel the success, be happy and thankful for the success. There is simply nothing else possible than success. This must be your psychic setting. Each day you must meditate about this aim. It must be so strong that you feel that it is already tangible. Full success must be your guiding light, your total trust, your motivation. Besides the right attitude you must be convinced that with every training your new ability will manifest more, better and stronger. Be totally convinced about your progress. Accept not a single doubt. See failure as necessary steps to success as you learn through it and your results get better in the end. You must be simply unstoppable.

In the third step you follow your training schedule with love, patience and an iron will power. You thank God and the spiritual world for every step of progress you make, for blessings and guidance. You keep your meditations about having already the new ability. Simulate with your imagination how you use the ability, how much joy it brings to do it, how fascinating the results are. Impregnate your subconsciousness with all these useful ideas and feelings of full success.

These three steps will lead to the manifestation of the new ability. But you have to understand that with the first step it needs a good amount of time to strengthen the idea of the new ability in such a way that it becomes denser and denser to manifest at last on the physical plane. A new ability means a change, transformation of structure on mental, astral and physical plane. This is comparable with the aim to run successfully a marathon. A marathon runner is different to a normal human. His muscles are developed. His lung volume has grown. His body appears fat free. His mental and psychic attitude has changed to master a marathon. At last he is a real marathon runner. A normal human cannot become a marathon runner from one day to the other as his mental, psychic and physical structure has to transform. This transformation process is nothing else than the manifestation of the "I am a marathon runner" idea from Akasha down to the physical plane. So it is normal and comprehensible that the ability to run a marathon cannot manifest directly in one training and also not in some trainings and not in one month. This is also valid for magical abilities. So in fact you have to go on in training with a positive attitude although the ability is not already available. Here it is important that you know that you are working on the transformation of yourself so that the ability can show up in a certain time of training. Normally you can expect first signs of the coming ability or the ability is already available for some seconds/minutes. It is just a process of growing, of development, of transformation and realization. When you understand this then you will be able to provide the necessary power and motivation to keep the training until full success manifests. This is the key and this must be understood. Believe in yourself and believe in the spiritual realms and their support.

For these reasons it is important to set a good and realistic plan for your training. Depending on your talents give yourself averagely three months of good training for a new ability. If this is not enough then continue your training and ask for divine help and insights. The spiritual world is very kind with true seekers but progress is in main a task of yourself and only in smaller parts of spiritual helpers. No one can do the training instead of you. And then – at last – know that there is a difference between a basically developed ability and real, professional mastership of an ability. A perfect handling of an ability can be only reached after years of usage and training. This all takes very much time and effort and so you will be already thankful for first success and applications. Learning magic is a matter of life times.

## DISSOLVING OF BLOCKADES IN AUTOHYPNOSIS

Just short: I present here a good technique for the use of autohypnosis. Nearly all humans and also nearly all students suffer from different kinds of blockades which appear on all planes, - on the mental, astral and physical plane. Blockades appear especially in the energy channels, the nadis or meridians and also in the chakras which work as energy pumps, processing energy suppliers and distributors. Blockades are in main dirty, ill and slimy energies which adhere and clog the energy channels and chakras. Blockades can also be negative thought patterns and negative emotional patterns. On the physical plane there can be structures which block the flow of metabolism. When there is somewhere a blockade then there are parts of the body/soul/mind which have too much energy (congestion) and there are parts which get not enough fresh energy (deficiency). The human microcosm is able to dissolve blockades by itself (in most cases) but it is necessary to lead the attention of the subconsciousness to the blockades. It is necessary to give the right impulse for self-clearing and self-healing processes. The reason for this is that the subconsciousness is very busy with "multitasking", with thousands of processes in the human body and with this its power is not focused on self-healing. Maybe the subconsciousness is focused on digestion or something else (while a lot of other processes are working parallel). So when you take consciously time for self-healing and dissolving of blockades then your subconsciousness gets the necessary impulse and focuses its attention and power on this subject. The good thing is that the subconsciousness knows exactly where the blockades and negative energies are. It also knows what to do to dissolve them. This is indeed a big advantage.

The technique itself is quite simple. Do it and observe what is happening on all three planes in your body in the next time (within three days). Certainly you can repeat the exercise. And certainly your subconsciousness and your body need time for this work, - give the process of clearing and healing enough time. It is possible that in a first exercise a good amount of blockades is cleared. In a second round further blockades are cleared and in a third round maybe the last problems are dissolved. This depends on your health and inner balance, - on your needs for clearing. Maybe all blockades are cleared already in a first exercise. It also depends on your abilities to get into a deep state of mind. It can be useful to repeat from time to time such an exercise as new problems can appear. Just follow your intuition as always.

The technique:

Get into your asana. Close your eyes. Now focus your attention on your breathing. Tell yourself (mentally) that with every exhalation you get "deeper and deeper" into a state of full relaxation, into a state of trance. Alternatively or additionally you can move with your mind from your feet through all body regions upwards to your head. Rest a short while in every body region and imagine or tell that the region is totally relaxed, warm and feeling well. With this you relax your whole body completely. After this deep relaxation and deepening of your trance you focus with your mind into the center of yourself respectively you set yourself into the Akasha point of your microcosm. Now tell your subconsciousness respectively imagine that all blockades on the mental plane, in your soul and in your body dissolve completely. Imagine that your subconsciousness starts a great process of self-clearing. Imagine how all blockades dissolve, vanish, break, how new, fresh energies flow and circulate, how your nadis are cleared, how your chakras start to work, start to participate in this great work of clearing, refreshing and healing, imagine how all bad energies dissolve and spit out of your chakras, how these energies are exhaled by your lungs, how your whole microcosm rebalances itself on all planes. Release all your blockades, release all bad thoughts, all bad emotions, all what hurts you. Imagine how all your wounds are healed, how you recover on all planes. Thank your subconsciousness for the good work. Tell it to go on until you are completely cleaned and healed. Then focus on the idea that you inhale fresh, healing energies which support your subconsciousness in its great work until you feel saturated with fresh, good energies. Then stay a while in observing the work in your body. Observe how you feel better and better. Then make the steps back into normal activity. Say to yourself that you count up to three and with the number three you open your eyes and you feel completely awake, refreshed, right here and right now. One – your breathing and your blood pressure increase to normal degrees. Two – you feel awake, refreshed, back into your physical body. Three – you open your eyes and you are back in the "normal" world – back from trance.

This is a very effective exercise with a lot of benefits for yourself. It helps in normal life, in health problems and in spiritual training. I wish and hope that this exercise is a true blessing for you. May it serve your progress!

## QUESTION: THOUGHT CONTROL AND MOTIVATION

The aim of the thought control exercise is to be able to observe your train of thoughts. The second aim is to experience that you and your thoughts are two different things. The third aim is later to get full control over what you think. Reaching these aims is important -

not the exercise itself! So please orientate yourself in main on the aims. If you fulfill the aims then you can go on.

Motivation for doing exercises only arises when your training is connected to desired aims. So indeed you must set yourself aims where you understand that the training is necessary to reach these aims. Only then you feel motivated to make it. The aim of the whole training is certainly to reach spiritual perfection/completeness and this is our natural-divine aim. So the training is just for you and certainly also a way of worshipping God and later serving God by divine missions. From a different perspective you could say that the abilities are already something to work for or that you can discover all secrets of life and God. So please search for your individual aims which are able to give you motivation, will and patience to master the path.

## SPACE CLEARING

From time to time it makes sense to clear your rooms, respectively your flat, house or space where you live and work. All kinds of mental and astral energies, thought patterns, emotions, energetic influences gather in rooms and connect to the living space, also to furniture, cloths and electric devices. Very often these energies are not of a positive type but in main exhausted energies, negative ones and also energies of disease can be found. Houses lack of a regular exchange of energies today and normally no one consciously blesses his house or charges it with fresh, positive energies. So a kind of hygiene of living spaces is recommended and useful.

A very powerful and also simple technique is to imagine violet light filling your living space, - room by room or the whole flat/house at once – as you like. Keep this concentration/imagination for several minutes. Imagine further on that this violet light permeates everything in your living space and that it dissolves all bad energies on all planes together with all bad influences, all bad connections and that it kills all negative beings (parasites). You can enhance this technique by imagining that this violet light permeates also your whole microcosm and dissolves here also all bad energies. The violet light cleans very good but at the same time it has a great healing power for yourself and other persons in the living space.

After doing this technique you will experience that the energetic atmosphere in your living space is really clean. You can feel it. If you like you can charge your rooms afterwards with fresh vital energy but this is not directly necessary. Something special is to imagine your living space into nature respectively a landscape you love. Then you can draw the special energy of this landscape into your rooms. In fact your rooms will have then the energetic quality of a forest or of a beach or whatever you love the most in nature. I did this once with a forest and it very amazing to experience.

Just have a try.

## FAMILY AND KARMA INHERITANCE

Today I want to speak about problems which are not your own but which you inherit from your parents respectively your family. This sounds quite strange but it is unfortunately a fact. Problems are passed on from generation to generation until someone solves it.

Imagine you are a teenager and you wonder about why you have certain problems in your personality, in behavior and life. You have negative characteristics where you would say that they are not your own, that they are not originally from you. You don't know where they come from but they appear somehow as a problem which you have to cope with. The more you are spiritually developed the easier you sense such things. You look at your personality and analyze what is originally you, what is from your grandparents, from your Mum, from your Dad, maybe from your uncle, aunt, etc. These are certainly positive and negative characteristics. Here the negative aspects are more important as they are obstacles in life.

Let's take an example. Imagine you suffer from choleric attacks and maybe you have had heavy depressions over long years, - both although you are not originally a choleric person and you have much joy in life. Normal people do not reflect on such things. They just think that it is in this way. But when you have a higher awareness of the circumstances in your life then you will discover that the choleric behavior is the same like your father shows and that the depressions have been passed on from your Mum in the time where your father has cheated her. Although these things are not yours, you suffer. This just as an example. Certainly you can discover that you have the same sense of humor like your uncle, that you are diligent like your grandfather, that you laugh like your grandma and so on. (It might be quite interesting to make a research.)

So how does this work and why? Mind, soul and body are analogue and completely connected. So the qualities, abilities and structures of mind and soul are reflected in the physical body. Due to this, by procreating a child, the information of father and mother build the basis for its personality and appearance. This aspect is the biological inheritance with the mixing of the DNA of the parents, - the physical aspect. Besides this aspect we have the phenomenon of mental and astral influence on a child by his social environment. This is in main with most power the family, - father and mother. A baby grows up in the mental and astral fields of the parents respectively in their energy atmosphere. The mental and emotional (astral) energy of the parents / family feeds the child and provides a growing of characteristics like it is present in the parents. So it is in main a matter of energetic nourishment. The problem is that the old personality which incarnates in a new physical body is just a mental being as the astral body together with the physical body has to develop itself. Something which is over years in development is malleable, needs to be nourished and it is open for influences. Children are very receptive for influences, especially from adults which appear in their eyes as omnipotent like gods. So adults have a model character for children and what adults say and do is reality and true for children. Children are very limited in their understanding and in their critical competences. They do not question and they do not reflect. Due to these characteristics of children they "inherit" very much from the parents and family on mental and astral plane. In puberty they try to get rid of the characteristics which are from their parents to discover their own personality. This is often only in parts successful. A lot of grown-ups suffer their whole life from negative influences of their parents. Beside the direct energetic influences parents give often negative suggestions to their children which they receive like in hypnosis, directly set and anchored in the subconsciousness. These are things like "You are too stupid to do this or that. You will never be successful in anything." And so on… In conclusion the incarnated mental personality has to withstand and to cope with the major influences of the family. It can be indeed a real fight for freedom, for self-development and self-determination. Such a fight can take years and often whole life times. Spiritual training is certainly a good way to deal with this.

A problematic energetic aspect is here that through the years strong energy connections between child and family have been built which work like highways for emotional exchange and certainly like real chains. Such connections can be dissolved or healed.

For the concerned person,- the child, a problem occurs which is like an alien, where you do not know where it comes from and how you can deal with it. For example imagine that in a former incarnation you were a warrior and now you are a normal person and you experience social fear. For an old warrior social fear is something he does not know and he does not know how to get rid of it. It is an alien characteristic which he received in his new incarnation from his Dad (just as an example). Or another example, - imagine you are originally a very successful personality but in this life you are blocked by the failure quality of your father. So these things are very hard to understand and to cope with. The next problem is that you pass such negative characteristics on to your own children when you are not able to heal yourself. I know several examples where children copy their parents in behavior and character and where this has led to real problems in their lives. This means quite often to mess up your own life because of the negative influences of your family and certainly because you were not able to cope with them.

On the other hand when you are strong in your personality then you can overcome such negative influences and settings.

From a spiritual point of view there is to say that there is a certain form of resonance between the new parents and the old mental personality which wants to incarnate. So in parts the parents fit mentally and emotionally with the new child but there are also other reasons to incarnate exactly in this family and not in another one. It is all quite complex with positive aspects and with negative ones which have to be balanced.

So in conclusion it makes sense to analyze your original personality, the "alien" parts of your family and to get rid of the negative aspects for a good life of freedom and self-determination.

As a last point – it makes sense to heal not only yourself but also your family members respectively your beloved ones for a lasting peace and harmony. As long as your family is not healed you are confronted with negative thoughts and emotions every time you meet them.

To get yourself healed and your beloved ones I recommend a simple technique. Get into your asana and treat all people of your social environment (family) and yourself in the same way: Focus on a person as a whole and then think that there is also the aura of the person, - the whole microcosm indeed. Now leave the physical appearance of the person and just concentrate on the idea of her/his microcosm (body with aura) – here just the idea, not the picture. Now imagine that the microcosm of the person is flooded, filled with violet Akasha light which permeates mind, soul, body, aura. Keep this imagination and command/imagine that this violet light dissolves all negative energies, all negative influences, all blockades, all ill energies and all negative connections on all planes in this microcosm. Additionally to this powerful clearing process the violet light supports deep self-healing processes on all planes. In this way the person is cleared and healed. You can / should repeat this work several times. You will experience how the persons will change to the positive. Expect surprises. Clear also their living space with violet light so that all negative energies dissolves in their rooms / flat. This is a necessary work. All these healing and clearing treatments will be a real spiritual service and a real blessing for your whole family and their internal relationships. Don´t forget to treat also yourself.

Similar treatments can be given for all kinds of social groups, - for your family, for your beloved ones, friends, at work, for the people you are in connection. You will experience a bright blessing everywhere.

It is indeed one of the best things you can do for yourself and your life.

## THE YEAR 2012

Dear fellows,

in a few days we enter 2012. Due to the latest news I want to speak about this new year and what might come. There are political powers which long for a third world war starting with the fight against the Iran. When the USA, Israel and the states of Europe start this war then Russia, China and others will take part but on the other side. And this means truly a world war. Certainly the Iran is not the real cause but just a way to start it. The reasons for this are diverse. Certainly the "New World Order" is one thing, another one is the idea that the appearance of a Mahdi or Messiah can be forced by this, also that a total destruction of main parts of the world provides new possibilities for a "reconstruction" and good business, etc. The problem is that the Satanists do not really like this idea as they all lose much. The alternative – the ecological terror – as a way to force and control people does not really work. So the Satanists have to improve their strategy. Sure is only that in 2012 major changes are foreseen to take place. So we can expect surprises. A leading Satanist has predicted this for 2012, - either the ecologic terror works or a third world war has to take place. But I guess they have to improvise respectively have to experience that their ideas are far away from reality.

Today further news appeared which are also very interesting. Scientists have developed a super virus which has the power to kill millions of people. If this is a fact is a different thing. In the news they wrote that this super virus should not get into the hands of terrorists as we have to expect then millions of dead people. So what should such an article tell us? First, that an artificial super virus has been developed. Second, that we should fear it together with terrorists. Third, we have to expect millions of dead. In "translation" this means that a kind of secret service will spread some kind of deadly substance among people to produce millions of dead in USA, Europe, Asia, maybe also Africa. Officially these will be as always "terrorists" and to fight them people have to sacrifice their rights for more control. This super pandemic fits perfectly into the plans of the Satanists and it was already advertised by an according movie at the cinemas.

Beside these beautiful ideas many civil wars can be expected in Europe but also in America and Asia. The financial systems are going to break down, also political systems. From this chaos something new will arise. The question is what. Chaos and lies are the fundaments of society today. Only order and truth can last.

I must say that the Satanists have made big mistakes and these mistakes are going to break their necks. Their work is quite unprofessional and their comprehension is too limited. I truly would enjoy to see them all accused and sentenced. Then the best part would be to let them undergo a spiritual clearing and healing treatment so that they understand in the end what they have done. This would be the most terrible punishment a human could think of.

My dear fellows please stay strong in your belief in yourself and in God. Keep good care for you and your beloved ones. Keep working for the light especially in the darkest hour. Equal to what will happen, - the spiritual realms will wait for us. Probably next year the old and eternal human values will count more than ever.

Let us hope for the best. May the eternal light bless us all with divine guidance and power to master all challenges which are waiting.

Yours, Ray


## LAWS, JUSTICE AND ORDER

The eternal light, the highest being has built creation on laws and principles. So creation is not a matter of arbitrariness but of divine will and laws. The description and use of these natural-divine laws is given in metaphysics, the science of qualities, powers and matter on the different planes of existence. The laws in creation are the basis for the order in and of creation. Order is always based on laws. With order justice appears. When a (human) spirit goes against the order of creation, - against his own order, against the laws of his own nature then the spirit experience justice as a necessary form of rebalancing what have been brought out of balance. Violating laws means causing imbalance, disharmony, chaos. As the natural-divine laws together with the natural-divine order cannot be separated from the individual being the violation of laws means to hurt yourself. This includes all forms of negative karma, fate. In the opposite this means that when you serve the laws, the natural-divine order then you receive the good fruits.

The (human) spirit uses different forms of embodiment, different forms of self-expression on the diverse planes of existence. The spirit as an Akasha principle is very flexible, quite unlimited, independent. When a spirit incarnates into a body on which plane ever then the spirit has to follow the laws of the plane of incarnation. Due to this we humans have problems to cope with the laws of the material plane as our spirit is not limited in this way. Indeed we have to learn the material laws to master life on this plane.

Beside these fundamental conditions there are two phenomena which are interesting. The first one is that spiritual masters know all laws of creation and have the power to use them for their purposes. This means that they are able to change reality, - a reality which is unchangeable by regarding only the laws of the according plane, respectively the limitations of the concerned undeveloped person. So the more you know and the more abilities you have the more you are able to change your reality. These operations are all based on the natural-divine laws and the order of creation. And with this they are lawful.

The second phenomenon deals with Asuras and Satanists which filter out and ignore everything which does not fit into their point of view, into their perception of the world. So they do not ask about laws, order or principles of creation. In contrary they orientate themselves on their own personality, on their own wishes, beliefs, ideas, emotions and ideologies. They truly think that they can give creation an own artificial order, own laws and certainly an own justice. This is pure nonsense. No one is able to withdraw himself from the natural-divine order and its justice. It is indeed remarkable to observe how they create laws for society which are not relevant for themselves. This does not work at all. In fact the divine laws are valid for all creatures without a single exception. Imagine you have mastered all steps of your spiritual development so that your nature has become divine nature and you are a respected authority in the macrocosm. Also in this spiritual perfection you are responsible for all your actions and you will have to regard the laws and order of creation. The eternal light will be above you and could punish you if necessary. (It should be clear that such a high developed master would never even think about to go against the eternal light or the natural-divine laws of creation.)

So never believe such funny ideas that someone is able to stand above the laws. The day of judgment will come for everyone.

You may wonder why so many Satanists seem to keep unpunished. This only appears in this way. One aspect is that some Satanists try to balance their evil behavior with "charity" and donations. Another aspect is that they have pacts with negative beings, demons which make it possible to do more evil without direct consequences. But for sure the punishment will come in this or another way, - in this incarnation or another one. Remember: "The mills of God grind slowly (but perfect!)".

## SPECIAL TECHNIQUE FOR AUTOHYPNOSIS

I have done some interesting experiments with autohypnosis. If you have a very big problem which you cannot solve with your normal consciousness then you can use the following technique:

Set yourself in the state of autohypnosis, trance respectively a deep state of relaxation. Then tell your subconsciousness to "cooperate" with divine omnipotence or other divine virtues to solve your problem. By doing this you connect yourself to divine sources of power, love and wisdom and with these superior energies much more is possible than with just your own energies or the surrounding vital energy.

So indeed you can work with magic in a state of hypnosis. Just do some experiments and try it.

## Help for Visual Imagination

Visual imagination can be a problem if the needed talents are missing or if the subject which has to be imagined is too complex. You can help yourself very much when you use paper and crayons to draw it. There is no need to be an artist. Just make a sketch to illustrate your subject. It helps very much for meditation and for magical operations. When you have made a picture of your idea, thoughts, subject then you have already a kind of mental picture to work with. You can also use the picture to work with it in meditation with open eyes.

Certainly when you train drawing and the process of making pictures from your ideas then imagination becomes easier. Maybe you know "mind maps". This business/study technique is indeed just a good way for meditation about a topic.

As always – just try!

## Tension and Power

The degree of effectiveness in magical operations is in main a matter of tension and power. It is a matter of quality, the degree of fineness/refinement and quantity, the amount of power. Imagine a normal human. He has maybe a radiance of one meter which means he has a normal level of vital energy. Now imagine that this person takes a rock crystal in one of his hands. The crystal is a natural collector and battery for vital energy. As the person gets in touch with this crystal the energy flows into his microcosm and further on increases the activity of several chakras. The result is that his energy level has increased up to maybe two or three meters radiance. So the person has much more energy (quantity) to realize his wishes or to give spiritual healings for example. When you do mystical training then you refine yourself to a higher energetic nature which is similar to light and high voltage. When your nature is very fine like light then your radiation is penetratingly and goes "very far". When you combine now a refined nature (quality) with a high level of power (quantity) then you are extremely "powerful" in everything you think, wish and do in magic. Your thoughts realize quickly. When you have this power not under absolute control then you can hurt yourself or others in shortest time (with bad ideas). So it is clear why inter alia a high positive-spiritual attitude is required for magical training. You prevent self-destruction and only with a real spiritual attitude you are able to melt with divine consciousness and divine virtues.

When you have reached high levels in the magical-mystical training then you can manifest divine consciousness and virtues in yourself at any time you want and certainly you are very refined and powerful already by your training. In former times it was common that high initiates have stayed in divine consciousness together with divine power, a high tension over longer times or also over the rest of their lives. This means they invoked their god-form and kept it by. This is known from spiritual masters in India but this is also the case for Jesus while he performed all his wonders. Wonders are only possible when you are in your divine consciousness together with divine virtues and powers. You experience yourself and your abilities as divine and so it is indeed.

In normal life today it is difficult to keep such a state as it is unknown here and not respected. In worst case you come into a lunatic asylum. In former times and still today in India it is respected. A last aspect is that your body, your energetic structure has to be able to cope with the enormous power and tension. When you are completely healthy and when you have a fit body then you can cope quite well with them. But in general one has to be careful with too much energy. It can lead to real problems with your nervous system.

Now you know what you need for performing wonders. Become a divine high voltage power station and then nearly nothing is impossible.

## THE MAGIC OF RESOURCES

In modern psychotherapy the term "resources" has an interesting meaning and use. Imagine you have a problem where you do not know how to cope with, where you miss the necessary insights, energies or characteristics. In the language of psychotherapy you lack of the necessary "resources". To solve your problem you must find the necessary resources and you must use them. For example you suffer from fears in a certain situation. This means that you lack of courage or self-confidence in this situation. This doesn´t mean that you permanently lack of courage or self-confidence. So in a psychotherapy treatment you can remind yourself on a situation where you experience yourself with courage, self-confidence. Then you can use this experience to connect your resources with the negative situation to experience it in a positive way – without fears. This is a magical operation for sure but called today psychotherapy of hypnotic treatment. The point is further on that you can use all kinds of resources for creating a positive experience in a formerly bad situation. These are your own experiences, witnessed experiences on TV or movies at the cinemas or from novels, tales, other people in life, etc. You probably know a situation where you were watching a movie thinking "The hero is very powerful and brave. He masters all challenges. I want to be like him." Or "He is a brilliant speaker. It would be great to be like him." Something like this. And indeed you can use these movie characters to imagine such characteristics, abilities for yourself, to get in touch with them, to feel them, to experience them. Imagine yourself as a hero for example to experience being brave, being a leader, being successful and so on. In some way it is "learning by following models". So when you have somewhere a kind of problem you can look for a fitting positive resource to change your reality, your perception, self-perception and you behavior.

Further aspects are here the magical melting with divine virtues, to experience yourself as one with God respectively your personal god-form. It is a change of reality, a change of self-experience. Then from the oldest shamanistic traditions we know that they melt with the spirit/idea of animals and their characteristics. This is certainly a wider topic than the use in psychotherapy as Shamans often become these animals on a higher plane. So it is a transformation, somehow comparable with the idea of werewolves. Transformation on mental and astral plane from one shape/body into another one is possible and known. The Shamans certainly follow inter alia the idea to take part in the special abilities of the animals. When you think of jaguar or a bear or an eagle, - they all have special characteristics, special powers and abilities. Although most of us are no Shamans you can use the ideas of animals as resources to enrich your character. Imagine you have to cope with a situation where you have to present yourself in a good way, where you should act with self-assurance. Now you can do a meditation before this where you imagine yourself as a lion taking part in his characteristics. A lion is powerful, a being of the sun sphere, full of self-confidence, like a king, with a strong assertiveness and so on. Here you can really imagine to be a lion. Imagine to act like a lion, to show your big teeth, to show a royal behavior, to show your immense and unchallenged power. When you are mentally prepared in this way then you should stand your presentation in society quite well. You have enriched your personality with qualities of a lion.

Useful animals are lions, tigers, eagles, hawks, horses and many others. Just think first about the wished for qualities and then choose a fitting animal to take part in his characteristics and powers. Certainly you can use also gods and goddesses, aspects of creation like mountains, streams or big trees and so on. There are no limits.

Have much fun!

## LOVE – A MASTER KEY

Only a very few words: Love is a really important key in the spiritual, magical, mystical development. Without love and its aspects thankfulness, humbleness, joy, etc. nothing can be reached. So if you want to make any progress of real value then love God, love all gods and goddesses, love all divine spirits, love your spiritual guide and your master, love your brothers and sisters, love your fellow creatures, love yourself, love all parts of yourself. Keep and care for relationships of true love with all beings. More is not really necessary to say. When you do so then the mysteries of love will unveil to you naturally.

People tend to forget about these fundamental things. Be wise and live it!

## THE HAWK WHO LIVED AMONG THE PIGEONS

Do you know the story of the hawk and the pigeons? Normally hawks and pigeons live separated and do not deal with each other. But once it happened that a young hawk grew up in a community of pigeons. He didn´t know that he was a hawk and his nature was different to the nature of the pigeons. Indeed the hawk thought that he was a pigeon himself - just looking somehow different. The pigeons wondered about the strange pigeon (hawk) among them. They did not understand why the hawk - the strange pigeon - was able to fly much better and higher than they were able to and they did not understand why he hunted for mice instead of eating seeds. So the relationship between the normal pigeons and the strange pigeon (hawk) was tensed, not easy although the hawk tried to be like a pigeon to be integrated in their community. Every day the hawk did his best to think, feel and behave like a pigeon but it did not work and it cost him much energy to play his role. He kept being a stranger which he did not understand. He became somehow ill because of this stress. He got irrational fears, felt blocked and he was unsatisfied. One day it happened that another hawk came along and wondered about the other hawk sitting among pigeons and making the same sounds like them. So he decided to fly to them and to talk to the pigeon imitating hawk. When the pigeons saw the coming big hawk they got anxious and flew away. The "pigeon-hawk" wondered that there was another strange pigeon like him. The big hawk came: "My friend, what are you doing among the pigeons and why do you behave like them?" "I am a pigeon myself." He answered. "No, you are not a pigeon; you are a hawk like me!" "A hawk?" "Yes, you are of a completely different nature than these pigeons. You must have been fallen out of your nest. Good that the pigeons have cared for you but you cannot live any longer among them. You must return to yourself,- to your own nature and your own way of living! Come with me. I teach you how to live as a master of the air, a highly respected, kingly bird of prey. You must live in an adequate way and follow your sense in life! Be yourself, follow your duty! Leave the pigeons behind!" The young hawk understood and his stress and illness vanished. He knew that the wrong way of life made him ill and that from this day on he would lead the life which was meant for him - as a respected master of the air.

What do you think - was the hawk right to follow his nature or should he has stayed as a strange pigeon among real pigeons?

# THE WORK OF LIGHT AND DARKNESS

I do not want to talk about all aspects of this topic as this would be really too much. I just want to focus on a few parts which are quite interesting to observe. Throughout the history of mankind the servants of light and the brothers of darkness have incarnated to cultivate their traditions, schools and certainly to educate new masters to keep their spirit alive. So indeed both sides have been active for their traditions worldwide throughout space and time independent from culture or religion. Both have kept their work in different forms, - in official movements, in secret societies and also camouflaged. They have had connections between the different planes of creation. This means down here on the material plane masters and aspirants have been working while on the astral plane and the mental plane their brothers have been keeping the connection to them for communication, guidance and influence. So it is in fact a form of network over the different planes of existence. It is in major parts the work behind the scenes to reach the aims of light and darkness.

One point is that it is possible to meet masters and creatures from the farthest past or that you discover that your secret society is led by such an old being. Maybe you discover old cults today where you think that they have gone thousand years ago already but indeed they are still alive. Certainly it is also possible to experience the atmosphere of old rituals on the higher planes while visiting the ruins of temples. Magic is everywhere. When you visit museums with old artifacts then you can feel their magic, their light and sometimes their darkness. This is also valid for old graves. In old cultures it was common to protect graves of high initiates with magic and spirits. So it can be quite dangerous to open such a grave and additionally the spirits of deceased can still live there. Especially when a culture turned to darkness with black magic and really bad happenings then still today much darkness and dark beings can be discovered there. On the other hand there are still enough temples or ruins where you can feel the great spirit of light from the golden times. In general it is recommendable to be full aware of what kind of things could be expected in old religious places, graves and museums with old artifacts. Secret societies of today still use very old magical buildings for high initiations. They meet there very old creatures, gods and high priests of declined ages. Besides this it is interesting that some adepts have prepared their physical bodies in graves and caves to outlast hundreds or thousands of years so that they can use them again for special missions.

There is so much magic in the world that it is incredible, in parts unbelievable but still reality. There is much hidden light but also immense danger from darkness. And so much is going on behind the scenes.

## PRIVILEGES

It is a privilege to be a human.

It is a privilege to be a god.

It is a double privilege to be a god-human.

Why?

It is a privilege to experience yourself as a limited human being.

It is a privilege to experience yourself as an unlimited divine being.

It is a double privilege to experience yourself as both, - limited and unlimited at the same time.

All three experiences are very precious and unique. So we human beings are indeed privileged to be able to make such experiences by our natural-spiritual development.

It is worth to meditate about this topic to comprehend and to appreciate what is given to us.

## BOOK RECOMMENDATION

Dear fellows,

I have studied many good books about psychology and psychological treatment for helping people. A big problem of psychology today is that the scientists do not really understand the nature of human beings. On the other hand they made useful research.

As magic is a matter of psychology, the science of mind and soul and its effects on behavior and mastership in life, every spiritual seeker should study psychological knowledge to understand himself and others better.

I have found a book of Kevin Hogan which represents the peak of psychological - useful - knowledge. The title might be a little bit misleading. It explains the human nature, consciousness and subconsciousness, human values and behavior and last but not least how to master your life regarding psychological aspects. And indeed it is a spiritual intention behind this book.

So if you have the money to get one then invest it for your own spiritual development and a better management of your life.

Here it is:

Kevin Hogan: Covert Hypnosis: An Operator´s Manual 2020

Ray

## PROGRESSION, IMAGINATION AND MASTERSHIP

In hypnotherapy there is a technique where you go back into your past to experience important situations again to solve problems in the presence. It is called regression. It is possible that you feel and act like a child in such a session like you did in the past where you have gone under hypnosis. Something similar is possible with your future. It is called progression. Set into your own future you experience yourself much older and maybe wiser as your future-self. It is possible that you say what happened in the last years as a review. The point is that you have changed in your character and that maybe new abilities or qualities are there – just because you are older. Imagine that you are in a long term martial arts training. Due to the hypnosis session you experience yourself ten years older. So now you are no longer a beginner in martial arts but an old grand master. This is a different experience, a different feeling and attitude. With such a progression technique you can connect from your presence to energies and experiences of your future. You know how it feels like to be a master and this already as a beginner. Besides a real progression into your own future you can use imagination to experience yourself as a master, - a master in magic, an enlightened, refined and powerful being. Just get into meditation and ask yourself: "How do I experience myself as a master? How does it feel like to be one?" The chances are good that you indeed get to know such a state, the qualities, the attitude of a master, maybe you get into contact with according spiritual powers and maybe you have impressions about how it is to have new abilities. With such impressions it is easier for you to focus on your spiritual development as you know what is waiting for you.

Beside these more general things there is one technique which I suggest to you for a better progress in developing abilities/qualities. It could be named "Creating the Master":

Your aim is to reach complete mastership in magic and mystic. This is the basis. One part of the technique is "result imagination" and the other part is "process imagination" (simulation).   Bardon suggests to imagine yourself having already reached your aim, - the wished for state. This is "result imagination". With this technique you vitalize the desired idea, image with mental energy and with emotional energy so that it manifests from the highest plane down to the material world. This can take a while and has to be repeated like watering a flower. "Process imagination" or simulation is the second part. Here you simulate in your imagination the wished for ability, quality/behavior or state in process of training/using. Indeed you create a new reality which supports the manifestation of your wish. We can say that it is a reality for your subconsciousness as it does not differentiate between imagination and "real" reality. In other words your imagined reality is real but on a different plane. Let´s take an example:

Clairvoyance

a)   Result imagination:
I am clairvoyant. I can see with my third eye everything I
wish to see on akashic, mental, astral and material plane
over time and space. There are no limitations for my third
eye. My third eye is in perfect condition, well trained and
brilliant in its perception. My view is clear and all-
permeating. I witness the wonders of creation. I can see
the dwellers of the different realms, the beings of the
elements, the gods and goddesses, the beings of nature,
the flows of energy. I can see everything. I see the spiritual
guides, the masters, the old prophets, the brothers and
sisters in the light. I witness the history of mankind and the
future. I discover the secrets of the pyramids, of old
temples and ruins. All mysteries are open now for my third
eye. I am omniscient like my father (God). I am a master of
magic and mysticism. It feels great. I am blessed. I am
thankful. I am a son (daughter) of God. And so on...

b)   Process imagination:
I am sitting in my asana, in a deep meditation state. I am
not clairvoyant so far but I simulate it to create the desired
reality which helps my subconsciousness to manifest it.
Imagination: I focus on my third eye and feel that it is
active and completely developed. My intention to see with
my third eye is already enough to activate the sense of
clairvoyance. I feel how my third eye and my throat chakra
become more active. My consciousness has a slight shift
and I see my own aura with its colors. I focus now on the
chakras. I see my active crown chakra and the inner chakra.
I see the golden and violet colors. I see how the divine
energy enters my head, my energy system and how it flows
through my nadis. I can see the big chakras but also the

smaller ones. I can see into my body, the energy of my organs...I have watched my whole microcosm. How fascinating it is. I am thankful and happy for this brilliant ability. My clairvoyance gets better and better each day of training. Now I return to my normal sight and I finish the meditation. And so on...

This was just a small example. The more creativity, fantasy you put into your imaginations the better you nourish your desired reality. Most important is that you take part in these meditations with 100% - live it! Integrate all your senses and your emotions to make it real, to vitalize it. See yourself, feel yourself, experience yourself in the desired state. When you combine both parts – result and process imagination and repeat it regularly then you do the best to manifest what you wish for. As a third part real active training is certainly necessary. You can compare this with the training of a weightlifter. Imagination is important but real training is certainly necessary. Magical abilities need training similar to muscles. Structure has to be built.

You can be sure that all necessary ideas and energies exist already somewhere in creation for your new abilities and that you connect to them by such a training. During your magical training you can put step by step new abilities and qualities to your vision of mastership and so you complete yourself, your image until you and your perfect state are one.

## SOMETHING CURIOUS

Maybe you have heard or read about experts who analyze the behavior of people to say if they lie or not. These experts use an interesting technique to find the right answer. They imitate the concerned person in gesture, posture and facial expression. Then they know the truth. A curios technique, isn´t it? In fact these experts use unconsciously an aid to transfer their consciousness into the concerned person as Bardon would say. In different words they connect their mind to the mind of the other person to get an insight, an impulse or impression about what they want to discover. This works. You can try it yourself.

Similar techniques are used in India to melt with gods and goddesses. They imitate the worshipped god in posture and gesture and in imagination they become one.

In psychology respectively in NLP the experts call the imitation or mirroring of their clients "pacing" to get into connection with them, into rapport, into resonance.

Magic can be discovered everywhere in life!

## MENTAL HEALTH

Today there are many different kinds of stress which have bad influences on mental, emotional and physical health. It is indeed not uncommon to experience real damage or massive problems because of too many hours of overtime, of too much work at monitors, too much stress with other people at work or at home and so on. Life has become a real source of permanent stress in many ways. On the other hand opportunities for relaxation and collecting fresh, positive energies are quite often missing. And so the degree of disharmony increases and consolidates. I personally know meantime several people in good age with real mental problems just because of too much work at PCs and the missing positive compensation. Where should this end? In a complete collapse around forty years of age? I can´t answers this but I hope that this is not going to happen.

Spiritual people who have a basic knowledge about chakras can work on their mental recovery with simple exercises. For mental health the head chakras are in main responsible. So you can heal yourself on the mental plane when you do concentration exercises with all your senses similar to Bardon´s work on the imagination skills. You can also concentrate directly on the head chakras. Equal to how you do it the activation of the chakras/senses lead to a clearing, refreshing and healing of the whole head respectively of your mind. Quite fast you will experience first positive results. Beside this work I recommend additionally a real deep relaxation which is only gained by a hypnotic treatment or by listening to Theta wave sounds. Such a deep relaxation is able to release the complete tension, stress of your body, also all kinds of energetic blockades. Such results can´t be gained by normal sleep!

Your emotional health you can restore by focusing on your heart chakra for deep inner peace and by concentration exercises on your solar plexus chakra as this chakra is the most damaged and polluted chakra of humans in general. So inner peace and clearing/healing of your solar plexus is good for your soul. The activation of your heart chakra increases also your immune system which is certainly also a very useful effect.

You can increase your physical health by concentration exercises on your foot chakras, your root chakra and your hand chakras. All these chakras supply fresh vital energy to your body. The root chakra is certainly the main chakra for energy supply. It belongs to the earth element but also to the fire element. When you are experienced with your Kundalini Shakti then you can use her to heal your body and to vitalize yourself. With some caution you can also concentrate on your navel chakra for improving your digestion. Too much concentration can lead to diarrhea. You can also use your hara chakra to increase your energy level respectively to strengthen your energetic matrix.

All in all it can make much sense to work on your recovery on all planes respectively to use the chakras or methods you individually need. A lot of can be done just with working with the Maha Shakti (Kundalini) sitting in your root chakra. Experience is good and useful. Otherwise just try but be careful. Have a loving attitude to this divine creative female power.

Last but not least it is amazing how much modern life can ruin your health in shortest time and on the other hand how effective you can treat yourself for recovery.

## About egoism

The phenomenon of egoism is well known today and certainly throughout all ages of mankind. How does it appear on the energetic level? The quality of egoism belongs to the solar plexus chakra/center in the human microcosm and to the sphere of the sun in the macrocosm. The solar plexus center is the individual self which experiences life in interaction with other individuals and creation. It is the core of the microcosm like the sun is the core of the macrocosm. Originally it is good and positive. It is a child with limited understanding. But due to the negative circumstances of life on earth this positive and kind self can become selfish, evil. On the energetic level this means that a healthy solar plexus center becomes dirty and too big in comparison to the other centers. With a healing treatment you can clean and balance this center. Another point is the relation of solar plexus chakra to heart chakra. The heart chakra is the opposite of the solar plexus chakra. So when you develop your heart chakra you develop altruism, selfless love, inner peace and so on. Your solar plexus, your self, will benefit from these energies and qualities as it will be nourished by them naturally. This takes place on the level of soul. On the mental level you increase your altruism and beyond personal interests behavior by the development of the crown chakra. This is also a kind of balancing of the solar plexus center. In the perfect state of the microcosm all centers are integrated with all their positive qualities and powers working perfectly together. We need the positive powers and qualities of the sun and we need the individual self to experience life. The sun, respectively the individual sun has an immense meaning for the whole.

Clearing, healing, refinement and integration are the master keys for human development. This is also valid for egoism.

## HEALING TECHNIQUE WITH AKASHA

I have found a nice healing technique. When you are a Quabbalist then you can charge a room with the E-O formula. It provides a great balancing, healing effect on those who are in the room respectively stay/sleep in the room for recovery. You can strengthen the formula by repeating the E maybe three times and then the O three times. Derived from this quabbalistic technique you can use a normal magical technique as follows: Load the room with normal Akasha. Then charge the room with vital energy quite strong. Now you can give the common commands how long the energies should stay in the room for example for three days and that the energies should support all self-healing processes of the persons who are in the room. Just the typical commands. It works also without commands – here just fix the energies in the room.

How does it work? The Akasha energy fills the room and permeates everything inside of the room including all persons. When you charge now the room additionally with vital energy or electromagnetic fluid (earth element) then this energy is able to permeate everything inside the room too. The human body uses the vital energy to heal itself. Thanks to the Akasha element the vital energy can reach all parts of the body and so blockades do not count. This is very healthy.

With this technique you can create spaces or zones in a flat where people, you or for example animals receive the necessary energies for a strong and deep self-healing. Certainly you can use this technique also for space clearing.

## Sometimes...

Sometimes I think that the world is an incredible lunatic asylum with amazing forms of flourishing psychiatric diseases. Like the futurologist Gerald Celente discovered and proclaimed, the leaders of mankind are in main psychopaths and sociopaths, in other words exactly those people we need for a happy and prosperous life in health and peace.

Sometimes I think that mankind is not composed of Homo sapiens as sapiens means something like being wise together with comprehension. And what is human today? Where are the human values which make life worth living? I think mankind is somehow composed of a diversity of animals with some kind of intelligence and human appearance. The human world seems to be a big zoo. How many animals do you have to face each day of your life?

Sometimes I think that the world is some kind of Muppet Show with many really strange Muppets. The only things which are missing are dancing, singing and the great fun they have.

And sometimes I think that I am in a never-never land where everyone is sleeping and dreaming his life instead of living it. At the moment it seems that people experience more nightmares than nice dreams.

Isn´t it a strange world we´re living in?

But what is this world really?

In fact our world is an amazing kindergarten with countless children, - good ones and bad ones, all lost in their games, all here for learning, for new experiences, for growing, - for growing up.

Our world is an incredible playground, full of adventures, strange happenings, tragedies and comedies, happiness and sadness.

And for a few our world is a university, - for those who have grown up through the years, for those who have become tired of sleeping, dreaming and playing games, - for those who have discovered the real treasures of life.

Let´s search for the real treasures!

## STUDY ABOUT SHEEP

"If you now ask, why there is no outcry, because that is just crazy, you should read a study by the University of Leeds. After that 95 percent of Europeans behave like sheep. We have a herd instinct and let us manipulate arbitrary. We constantly look only what others do, and do not want to stand out in the herd."

This is an extract of an article by Dr. Udo Ulfkotte from 20/01/2012. This study from Leeds says it all. Not more needs to be said to show the reasons for the circumstances of life we experience today. And when Gerald Celente proclaims that all leaders are in main psychopaths and sociopaths then you know where the sheep are moving to.

## PROGRESS BOOSTER FOR MAGICAL DEVELOPMENT

For several years now I have been writing about spiritual development, magic and mystic. My intention was always to give hints for an easier access to the spiritual-magical world, to the training of Bardon. I have written quite much in this time. The problem to access the training respectively the unfamiliar world of magic certainly still exists for many seekers and beginners as the materialistic philosophy has separated us from God and creation. In former times when spirituality, gods and spirits where something normal people had a different attitude and with this a better access to spiritual development. Seekers looked for a master / guru and followed him. They were receptive for the higher teachings and they were willing to subordinate themselves to the divine spirit of the master. Today this is all lost. Today a seeker has to work on his own, has to differentiate alone between light and darkness, right and wrong. In comparison to the spiritual glory of the former days we now live at the bottom of darkness, - no guru, no help, no guidance. Certainly in the past there were negative aspects too and today we have positive ones like masses of knowledge of all kinds of traditions and a free choice which way we want to take. I personally prefer the old days but they are gone and we have to cope with the conditions of today. I can only say that those are blessed who have experienced the guidance and care of a real guru.

But back to the topic: The challenge today is to make progress on the path in an acceptable frame of time and effort. (Here I presume that the seeker is really ready for spiritual development and fulfills all requirements. Without this all effort is senseless.) The training consists in fact of two parts. One part is the active training itself and the second part is the use of the subconsciousness for progress. This second part has a really great meaning but is underestimated quite often today. It is somehow if you try to make the path on only one leg although you have two. Now the "booster" is to use the subconsciousness to the maximum for an optimized progress. Here are a few possibilities:

1. You use autosuggestion daily to master all new abilities and wished for qualities. You must use autosuggestion with much will power and emotions, with strong belief and all this like a powerful meditation. Alternatively you set yourself into your subconsciousness and set there the seeds in a passive way. So indeed we have two forms here, - an active one and a passive one. It is up to you how you do it.

2. You learn autohypnosis to reach really deep states of consciousness and then you plant the seeds of new abilities in form of normal autosuggestion or in form of a

meditation (simulation). You can enhance this with using rituals for the deep state of mind and rituals, gestures, so called triggers for the new abilities. These triggers, rituals work like a switch to activate what you wish to.

3.  You use autohypnosis together with for example Neuroprogrammer which produces special mind waves for deep states of consciousness. This is very effective and easy. Have a look here:
    http://www.transparentcorp.com/products/np/index.php

4.  You go to a hypnotist you trust and tell him what you wish for. Together you work out a good suggestion text and a ritual / trigger to activate the wished for ability. This is very easy and very effective. Just make sure to consult a real hypnotherapist with a comprehensive education. The only problem is that you have to pay the hypnotist. A hypnotist can help you to get into deeper states of mind quite easy and he can help you to manifest new abilities very effective. Certainly you must continue your active training but this can be a great help. I know people who have gained many "magical" abilities just by the help of professional hypnotists. The point here is simply that due to hypnotic treatment you get in best case direct access to the Akasha plane of the person and what you plant there has great power to realize. What is called hypnosis is indeed a mixture of influencing the subconsciousness and the personal Akasha. It is about creating new realities.

Probably I will publish in this year a book full of worked out auto hypnotic suggestions for nearly all ten steps of Bardon´s Initiation into Hermetics. With these "autosuggestions" you will develop all useful abilities and all necessary characteristics. But certainly you can do so also on yourself.

Then I will probably start my own office for hypnotic coaching maybe at the end of spring which will include workshops for spiritual development and officially named parapsychological research where people can develop higher abilities with hypnosis.

So an interesting time is coming for me. It is possible that I offer also workshops in English. Let´s see. [Meanwhile I have started it and if you are interested you can send me an email.]

In conclusion if you want to make as much progress as possible in the training then use a technique of hypnosis and integrate the power of your subconsciousness. Later in training you can certainly also use the Akasha element and the shift into the Akasha point to optimize your results.

Everyone on earth has to pay much for the opportunity to be here and to make experiences, progress. So use this precious time to get the best out of it. People always start to regret the opportunities they have missed short before their death or after. I hope you will smile and be satisfied with what you have done with your time.

## A CASE OF KARMA

I have discovered recently an interesting case of karma which I want to share with you. It is an example how things can develop from one incarnation to the next one. It is about a person I have known in my youth, a kind of friend. He was the youngest child of about 5 siblings as far as I remember. We went together to school. He was very intelligent but he had big problems at school as he was often absent because of health problems. One day he was forced to leave school. After this he visited about 6 different schools spread in the area

97

where he lived. He never finished any kind of school. The years went by and then he was too old for school and not a single school accepted him. So he became unemployed living from unemployment benefit. During this time he became really fat. His problems increased further on and he was forced to get treatment in a lunatic asylum. All his rights were lost to a guardian which was set by court. Several times he tried to kill himself. If he is still alive I don't know.

So in fact this was a real tragedy. With his high intelligence he could have studied at university to experience a blessed life in wealth and happiness. You might ask why this did not happen. I will explain it. Beside his high intelligence he was someone who needed to be pampered and on the other side who was a little tyrant. He was born in a big family with a mother who was overstrained with strange ideas about health care and medicine and a father who was overstrained by the whole family with a tendency to aggression. His brothers where quite chaotic in their behavior and so the whole family was not "all right". His mother pampered him very much and took care that he drank much milk and fruit juices with sugar substitutes – "health care". From this overdose of lactose and sugar substitutes he had permanent problems with digestion. Due to this he had to go to several doctors who all were not able to help him as the problem was not his body but his wrong nourishment. And certainly due to this he missed school quite often. This problem was already bad enough but his mother who liked to read books about medicine came to the conclusion that her son had a problem with the metabolism of his brain, - which cannot be proved. So day by day she suggested to him that he is ill – brain and digestion. And so the evil got started and increased from year to year. Indeed he was completely dependent from his mother and he never started to grow up. He kept being a child.

Again – a real tragedy. Recently I got unexpected insights in this problem. I had the vision that in a former life, - his last incarnation, he was a man of wealth, - due to his high intelligence and talents. So he was able to pay people to care for him in his household and so on. In fact he was really pampered and all was done for him, all his wishes were fulfilled. The problem was that he mistreated those who pampered and served him. He was a little tyrant already in this life. He behaved like a child without real responsibility.

In this incarnation the problems have increased and he became "mistreated" by his mother, the person who pampered him the most, - indeed too much, too unhealthy. Additionally he became more a helpless child neglecting responsibility completely.

This is how karma can work and often does. What has happened? The behavior of the concerned person was strengthened in the last incarnation. It was not changed or balanced. In this incarnation the energies, - mental, emotional energies and patterns of behavior increased further on and were brought to a full-grown state with all consequences. The concerned person is forced to learn from what he did. He is forced to change his behavior, forced to balance himself and his life.

Regarding karma we can in general observe that things start with little energy, then the energies grow and unfold in specific manifestations and in a last step the energies reach a final state. Then a process of balancing, of a new start has to follow. The accumulation of karma to what we call fate is indeed comparable with the growing of a plant, - first it is seed, then a growing plant and at last it is fully grown, ready for spreading new seeds. When bad karma, a "bad plant" is small then you can cut or defeat it easily but when it is big and grown then it is hard and when it has spread new seeds then you have a big problem. Big problems we call bad fate.

Wise are those who keep care for their garden. Cultivate the good plants and cut early the bad ones.

## DIRECT KNOWLEDGE

Spiritual training provides a great range of very special abilities. One great ability is what is known as "directly knowing" or "direct knowledge". It is a form of intuition, of superior perception. Imagine someone asks you something and without any effort you know directly the answer. Indeed it is a matter of the divine omniscience which manifests by spiritual maturity. It is in main a quality of the crown chakra. "Direct knowledge" is very amazing when you face a complex problem and you directly perceive the hidden cause respectively the solution which is within. Fascinating is also that the comprehension is instantly in your mind, - in a split second, and additionally in big size. This means that it is not a single idea which enters your mind but "a whole story", a complex insight.

Certainly everyone should work on this great ability, on divine omniscience or "directly knowing". One part is the high maturity, the other one is training as you know it from the development of your higher senses.

## THE DIVINE GARDEN

Did you know that God is a gardener? Indeed God is a passionate gardener. His garden provides the greatest diversity of beautiful flowers. Everyday a soft wind caresses gently the flowers, a gentle rain cares for refreshment and the divine sun nourishes them. The atmosphere is divine and filled with love. And when the divine sun smiles down to the beautiful flowers then the flowers smile back in joy. This is the divine garden. And do you know the secret of the divine garden? The beautiful flowers are human souls for whom God cares every day with love, so that they grow and unfold to divine beauty. In the earth of the garden there are the unawakened souls, the sleeping and dreaming children of God. But one day they all awake and break through the surface to see the vast blue sky and the wonderful light of the divine sun. And the more they grow the more they unfold their beauty. And do you want to know another secret? You are one of the flowers which already unfold their blossoms. Isn´t this wonderful? To be a flower in the garden of God. And to receive the loving care of the great gardener every day?!

## THE BLACK TOURMALINE

This stone is traditionally used for protection, - against negative influences and black magic attacks. I did some experiments with black tourmaline stones and want to share my experiences. First of all the stone or crystal is something special as it appears black but has at the same time crystalline qualities regarding the reflection and also the reception of light. This depends on how rays of light fall on the stone, - the angle. Fascinating is also that the stone has a slightly visible violet shine. And then, the stone is known for its ability to charge electricity to some degree. Translated onto the energetic level this means that the stone charges itself with light, - with all color energies and is of akashic (black color) and electric fluid nature, - light is electric as you remember. And indeed so it works. When you wear such a stone then to your normal energy spectrum black Akasha energy and electric fluid energy are added. The Akasha energy bridges blockades and dissolves them in your energy system and the electric fluid supports this work and additionally increases healing processes and the natural shielding function of your radiation. So in conclusion such a crystal can be quite useful for clearing, healing and protection purposes. You can clear such a stone with spirit (alcohol) for example and you can charge it in the sunlight.

I personally experienced that two tourmaline crystals which I have worn in my pockets have increased and dissolved bad headaches and other blockades, bad energies. The black tourmaline has also a hidden connection / analogy with the solar plexus chakra. So you can put a crystal on this point and examine what happens. Look up the quabbalistic letter "U" and then you know what I mean. The effects of this stone and other crystals depend also on your level of energy and your refinement and also your ability to feel the flow of energy in your system. Very raw and dense people probably do not feel much and vice versa.

A general warning about the use of crystals: They work like batteries and they provide extra energy for the human energy system. This can be good and useful but this can be also too much or the wrong quality. Crystals often activate the deeper chakras. If this is too much and too long then it can be quite unhealthy. There are cases where people got ill from too many crystals and too much use of them. So please be careful and use crystals only with a certain purpose.

In general clear them from time to time, also recharge them in the sunlight and don´t forget that you can really program them so that they fulfill your wishes.

If you like you can study crystal healing, - the right use of stones for higher purposes. It is quite interesting.

## Spiritual proclamation

Some hundred years ago (it feels like this) I have written about the importance of a spiritual vow. Such a vow means to call on God and the positive hierarchy including spiritual masters, brothers and sisters on the path, spiritual guides, then the so called angels and higher beings like gods and goddesses and so on to say that you are ready to start your own spiritual journey to reach your highest aims at all costs and that you expect divine support to master the path. Such a vow has life changing powers and serious consequences. It means to balance your karma account, to dissolve your debts and to work on progress, - for spiritual, good fruits.

A vow is somehow similar to make a call to a travel agency and to book your journey without the possibility of withdrawal. So in fact your destination is determined and you have to pay for it but you will certainly reach your aim.

What could you do further on? You can assure yourself that all participants of the journey are going to help and support you so that you reach your destination in the best possible way. On holidays you do this with kindness and a good tip.

For the spiritual journey it works different. I have named it "proclamation". So after having made a good vow you can make a good proclamation. The basis is that you as a human being are foreseen to undergo a natural evolution respectively a spiritual development which normally takes uncountable incarnations but can be shortened by spiritual training. So indeed this is your natural purpose and also your right. And you can proclaim this right and all which is related with it. This means nothing else than that all beings of the positive hierarchy can and have to support you in your personal, spiritual development (!) And it means that the negative hierarchy has to respect you in your project, - further on the negative hierarchy can/has to support you by dissolving blockades on the path. Buddhists and Hindus use demons or negative gods/goddesses to get rid of illusions, negative qualities and so on.

All these things you can use for making good progress on the path. You can pack it into a good proclamation. It should contain the following:

1. Address your proclamation to:
   - God (the highest being)
   - The divine spirits (archangels and angels)
   - Gods and goddesses
   - Spiritual masters
   - Spiritual guides
   - Spiritual brothers and sisters
   - All good beings in creation (the four realms)
2. The content:
   - Ask for support
   - Ask for protection
   - Ask for the dissolution of all obstacles, chains, bad karma – all what hinders you from success, progress and a lawful, fulfilled life (a happy and blessed life does not interfere with spiritual progress and is simply a side effect of receiving the natural abundance of creation)
   - Ask for divine intuition and inspiration – divine guidance so that you learn and comprehend better

- Ask for fortune and blessings (life does not have to be hard and unbearable, - this is often a matter of karma balancing)
- Ask for higher teachings and empowerment, - abishekas
- Ask for meeting the right people and beings in life for progress
- And don´t forget to ask for support for your material life, for your job, your family and so on. Only when these material things are in a good condition you have the necessary resources to make good progress.
- And maybe I have forgot something, - so think well if you have everything for your proclamation
3. Then thank all beings for their support and help to master the path.

This all works only when you have made a spiritual vow before respectively when you have decided to work on your spiritual development as it is foreseen for you as a human being – true and high spiritual aims!

As long as you are not wholehearted dedicated to the spiritual path to perfection equal to your own tradition then you won´t get the full support of the spiritual realms.

Speak your proclamation from your heart. If you can/like you can set yourself into the Akasha or charge yourself, your room with Akasha with the idea that everyone will hear you.

(Nita Hickok provides something more or less similar with a focus on healing and clearing. You can ask her directly if you want further information. She calls it covenant.)

In general all old traditions have something like I have described as a vow and as a proclamation. Indeed they have very specific vows for very specific steps of development and initiation. Something individual and generalized works also well today, especially for those who study Bardon.

## TRAVELING INTO TRANCE

Spiritual respectively magic-mystical work is a matter of mind and soul, not of the physical body. And so all what we do takes place on the higher planes. The small problem which comes along with this is that our mind is focused on the material plane, on the material world around us and therefore we have to withdraw our mind and senses from the material world to the "inner" world, the mental and astral plane. It is often called inner world just because we close our eyes and withdraw ourselves from the "outer" world. In fact "inner world" is a misleading term and not useful. So we have to shift the process of experiencing (perception, thinking, feeling and behavior) from one plane to another plane of existence. This shift takes place every day naturally, - each time we go to sleep the consciousness shifts from the material world to the "dream world" – the higher planes. When you observe the brainwaves then you can see that there is a state of activity when you are awake, then by falling asleep the brain activity reduces and when you are in a state of dreaming your brainwaves reach an level of activity similar to the state of being awake. So falling asleep means to make the shift from the material plane to the higher planes. Here the problem is that we obviously cannot really control this to use it for training and the dream state is a matter of the subconsciousness as it controls it. Lucid dreaming is a possibility to take a certain degree of your normal consciousness into the dream state for self-controlled action. But this is not easy and from my point of view the subconsciousness has still too much control (which is not useful). I know "magicians" who use this technique and got trapped in illusions.

When you undergo a spiritual training with a lot of exercises in meditation then you get automatically used to deeper states of consciousness where you have withdrawn your senses and your experiencing from the material world to the higher planes. Here it is just a matter of training and repetition. The problem here can be that the shifting process takes place unconsciously, automatically, - so you do it but you are not aware of it or how you do it. And maybe you have problems to reach really deep states of consciousness, - deep trance where your experiencing is completely shifted to the higher planes.

Beside special techniques for trance like dancing, music, etc. you can set yourself consciously into deep trance just by following an easy strategy. It is a technique which is used for hypnotic treatment. The idea is to keep the mind busy by activating all senses in rotation. You can create an autosuggestion text which you record for yourself and play for training sessions or you just memorize the few main points and do it by yourself.

The shift of consciousness is called "induction", then the meditation or training session starts and at last you have to get back in your normal state of consciousness. All in all three parts.

Points for the induction:

- Focus on your breathing, how you inhale and exhale, take some deep breaths and imagine that you fall deeper and deeper into trance with every breath you take
- Focus on your hands, how do they feel like, on your fingers
- Focus on your feet, how they feel

- Focus on a wave of relaxation which flows and spreads in your whole body, feel it in all parts of your body, feel how you release all stress
- Imagine a place you love, focus on the feeling to be there, what can you see, what can you hear
- Focus on your head, how does it feel, can you release stress here
- Imagine listening to your favorite music and enjoy it
- Calculate something, maybe sum up the numbers of the actual date
- Imagine yourself in a good situation of the recent past
- Feel how relaxed you are
- Imagine a fragrance you like
- Etc.

Here it is just important to keep your senses and all parts of your brain busy and this in rotation. Doing this you will shift automatically into a deep state of trance and then you can do your training. You can also just imagine yourself in a good situation where you use all your senses. But first relax your whole body.

After your meditation you have to come back to the material realm. Here it is good to follow these points:

- Your breathing gets to a normal level (take some deep breaths)
- Your blood pressure gets to a normal level
- Feel more and more your physical body
- Feel how vitality comes back into your body
- Move your feet, your arms, make fists
- After a few minutes open your eyes
- Do a few physical exercises

After a while of training this induction you can anchor your deep trance state with a symbol, gesture, mudra, sign, ritual, etc. which means that whenever you use it then you will automatically enter the deep trance. Then you need no long induction. The anchor respectively ritual has to be trained and repeated several times for good function.

Just try and make good experiences.

## WHERE BARDON´S SYSTEM LEADS TO

Most students do not understand the greatness of the effects of Bardon´s training. I mean here especially the insights and abilities in comparison to the degree of refinement of normal science, religion and human powers. By coincidence I have found some nice and absolutely true sentences about this topic on the website of William Mistele. Under the headline *"Top Ten Reasons Franz Bardon Students Do Not Totally and Completely Master Chapter Three in Initiation into Hermetics"* he shows what I mean. I have underlined the sentences. The text itself shows a great sense of humor but also of truth. The whole text can be found on his website and certainly his work should be studied by every true student of Bardon. Here are the excerpts:

*"9. I practiced Bardon for two weeks and I still could not levitate, astral travel, evoke a spirit, or light a candle with my mind. This system sucks.*

*(Light a candle with your mind? That specific accomplishment would give you absolute power over all nations on earth. Any president or*

*dictator would serve only with your permission.* The angels rejoice that you found the training boring.)

7. I need rank, man. I need to feel important. Give me some degrees like the 32 degrees in the Masons or at least some really neat colored robes, even a secret hand shake would help. Maybe a Bardon sigil I would pin on my shirt so others would know that I am one of them?

(There are no excuses for failure, no exemptions allowed. The system belongs to Saturn--for Saturn, there are no advanced souls. We are all exactly equal. The goal is consciousness without attachment to mental substance--ideas, beliefs, philosophies, etc.; Astral energy--emotional attachments, or social identity--your role in society. Only kindness exists for Saturn because it annihilates all other attachment. Get with the program, dump that ego, and learn to be kind to just about everyone you meet. Idiot.)

4. Demons from past life, my own, or my family karma (e.g., Nazi parents) interfere with my practice.

(A sense of wonder and awe about the beauty of life preempt all karma of every conceivable kind. Make the exercises playful and full of delight. The darkness will flee from you because you now possess the supreme ultimate weapon, Pashupata, which Shiva gave to the warrior Arjuna. Its true name is joy.)

3. I did the vitality body breathing exercises. I got it man. I am cool, I mean, radiant with light and life force whenever I want. Isn't that neat?

(Chapter three appendix: "After repeated exercises you will be able to emit your vital power for miles." Oh, you got that too? Let me be the first then to congratulate you. *You have just attained physical immortality! Your aura literally shines like and embodies the spirits of the sun.)*

2. I got the five minute no thoughts entering my mind thing. Now you want what? Thirty minutes no disturbances when meditating? No way, dude.

*(You got five minutes no thoughts? Let me be the first to congratulate you- you have just surpassed almost every Zen master on earth. Now then, a half hour of no thoughts will allow you at will to contact with ease any spirit in the solar system. Just focus on a spirit and you have a direct, undeniable link. Ask a question. With your silent, empty mind its response will appear with perfect clarity.)*

1. I got the magical equilibrium early on. Big deal. You saying I have to work more?

*(It is impossible to attain magical equilibrium as Bardon lays it out. Human beings do not know what the water element is. A balanced and healthy social personality is not the same as one's magical identity. In Bardon's third book, he goes into great detail about how to master the four elements in the astral body. You will need full consciousness of the intricate psychology and magical properties of each element in order to totally and completely master chapter three. Oh, you did that already? Congratulations, you now know more about psychology than all psychologists on earth.)"*

> Do you understand what I mean? With a magical education you go beyond human achievements! You go beyond the ideas of the avant-garde in all disciplines. You go beyond all limitations! It is very useful to comprehend these consequences for yourself, for your life and also your profession.

## Special Self-Healing Technique

There exists a variety of self-healing techniques which access the healing process from different points of view respectively from a different focus. I want to describe one special technique which is quite simple but also very powerful. I must admit that this technique can have unwished side effects which have to be balanced if they occur. More about this later.

Get into your asana with a straight spine and head. Take some breaths and relax. Focus your attention now on your crown chakra. In this way you activate this center and gateway for divine energies. When you feel a good degree of activation then keep a part of your concentration on your crown chakra and spread your concentration on your whole body and just be. This means complete stillness of mind and full awareness of your whole body, - your whole microcosm. With this you lead the high spiritual energies from your crown chakra down into your body. Keep it. You will experience that other chakras become active too and you will experience that everywhere where you have problems of health like blockades, disharmonies, ill energies, etc. strong self-healing and -clearing processes start. Focus on and feel especially your crown chakra, ajna chakra, throat chakra and heart chakra. Just be. You can add to this process the idea of perfect health on all three planes. Here you can think that the divine state means also complete health and as you charge yourself with divine energies you take part in divine health. You can also imagine or feel yourself like a golden Buddha, - a perfect, divine being. If you have special problems then you can lead your concentration or focus to these areas to increase the self-healing process there additionally.

So what is happening when you use this technique? The crown chakra is the highest and most divine center in the human microcosm and it is also the gateway for divine energies. These energies are very intelligent to say it simple and of a high electrical nature. When you set yourself into stillness of mind and spread your awareness over your whole body then you flood yourself with these high powers and the intention of these high powers is to cause full harmony, - the perfect, divine state. The intelligent electrical high frequency spiritual power breaks all kind of ill energies and blockades immediately and it optimizes the function of the chakra-nadi-system. The powers of the crown chakra are often used for superior healing treatments, also to kill/dissolve energetic parasites and to shield a patient against negative influences.

A side effect can be to feel overcharged, - too much high frequency which your nerve system cannot cope with. In this case you can charge yourself with earth element which supports the healing too. You can do also physical exercises or take a salt bath.

As always do some experiments and observe how you experience it. The use of the crown chakra energies is very effective, simple and useful. There are a few further techniques to transmit such energies to other people for healing but also to create powerful elementals. A student of magic can discover such things on his own.


## THE PROBLEM OF BARDON´S TRAINING

A student complains about the difficulties to master the training without a teacher. My answer:

I understand this problem very well. There is no greater thing than to have a real authentic master. A real master does not only teach you individually but he also cares like the best friend you can have. It is in fact the greatest relationship human beings can experience.

In some parts of the world something like this still exists but for such a universal and complex system of development it is very hard to find a sophisticated master (who has time to care for you).

I understand also very well that every beginner of Bardon´s system is quite bothered to feel left alone without help and guidance. It is indeed not the best case but a hard and challenging case, for some the worst case. I am not happy with this.

A more or less unspoken fact is that those who are successful in Bardon´s training are in most cases people who are born magicians or have accomplished a long spiritual training in former life times. So indeed holy and enlightened people use Bardon´s instructions to develop further on to perfection. For more or less "normal" people the pure Bardon teachings are in main too hard, too challenging. So without a former spiritual career it can be really hard to make progress with Bardon without help. This is a quite unhappy situation.

When I observe the Bardon groups in the internet where people discuss things they do not really understand then I must say that this is also very unfortunate as they confuse others more than they help comprehending.

I personally cannot change these things but I try to support all genuine students. Around March this year I will start my work as a hypnotist-coach for life and business. Then I will offer seminars for spiritual development on the basis of Bardon with much background knowledge and hypnotic treatments for success in the exercises. And certainly I will work on the flaws and blockades of the student to enable progress. I think that this will be a real help and more cannot be given.

So certainly you are welcome to take part in such seminars. I will also teach techniques how you can work in a most effective way on new skills and positive characteristics.

The only question will be how to organize these things for the English speaking students as normally my seminars will be in German.

Let´s see.

Ray

PS: I have launched meanwhile my business and genuine spiritual students of the Bardon system are welcome to take part in my workshops. Just contact me via email for more information.

## MERGING WITH THE SPHERES

The superordinated aim of the spiritual development is the adaption of the microcosm to the macrocosm regarding its qualities, powers and perfect harmony. In the Jewish tradition this is compared with an celestial man, the ideal human being called Adam Kadmon, the macrocosmic vision of the microcosmic man.

And indeed nearly the whole training of Bardon deals with the refinement of the energetic structure of the student towards macrocosmic degrees. All breathing techniques equal if it is vital energy or the four elements, Akasha, the fluids and later the energies of the spheres and the quabbalistic powers, - all serve the same aim, the refinement of the human nature to highest degrees. It is real alchemistic work.

In his second book about the spheres Bardon does not clearly point at it but the charging of your mental body with the energies of the different spheres has a deep effect for the refinement of your nature. Later the quabbalistic-mystical training is the crown of refinement.

Beside these techniques I want to focus on two things:

As soon as you are able to connect to the spheres you can do breathing exercises with the very special energies of the spheres in your whole body and then in the according body regions and then in the according organs like you know it from other exercises. For this exercise look up the characteristics of the spheres and their energies. Such an exercise will do a lot of good for your refinement and your connection with the macrocosm.

Then a second technique for meditation. This is a high divine macrocosmic meditation. Study the spheres and their function, qualities and powers well and then meditate that you are one with sphere after sphere. And later you are the macrocosm with all spheres. This means you are one with the solar system we live in. Remember that your microcosm is spherical itself. (With the sun – solar plexus in the center.) This meditation can be mind-blowing and you will experience the resonance between the spheres and your organs respectively body regions.

The first exercise will provide much good for you already and I recommend it for your refinement. This already without the idea to visit spheres and spirits.

In this way you become indeed the celestial human being, the Adam Kadmon of the Jewish tradition.

## DISCUSSING MASTERSHIP AND ENLIGHTENMENT

Recently there was a "fascinating" discussion in one of the Bardon forums in the internet. The topic was "Who has mastered one or more books of Bardon and who not and how you know if you did so". In the internet there are often "fascinating" discussions. There are people who discuss the true names of angels and the right hierarchy. People discuss about the nature of God. People love to discuss what they do not know nor ever have experienced. And so they discuss their opinions but do not talk about reality. I understand that this is a way of entertainment and fighting boredom but there is no deeper sense in it besides feeding the ego and pigeonhole thinking.

People who have reached a good degree of spiritual mastership feel no need to talk about it as it has no consequences for others. You can only compare your degree of mastership in an ability to learn eventually how to refine it and you can exchange your experiences in one topic. But this makes only sense for people who have more or less the same degree of progress.

What happens when "mastership" and such things are discussed? People tend to blow up their ego and others tend to adulate them. And often the wrong ones are admired as superior masters where you can die of laughter if it was not as sad.

Simply said it is the tragedy of the internet forums. So much nonsense, so much misleading information, so many dull discussion, so much lacking of experience and true knowledge, so much ego, - all in all more disappointing than anything else. And when I see the very few genuine people there trying to give good arguments, trying to have a good influence on the forum, - they are unheard, ignored and taken on a ride. And for what?

What said Jesus? Don´t throw pearls to the pigs as they do not perceive their value. There is so much wisdom inside.

## ENVIRONMENTAL POLLUTION IN BARDON FORUMS

I think I have written already some sentences about this pollution problem in the internet. But, as it is a serious problem, I want to focus on some points to prevent major damage. I must admit that I follow in parts these funny discussions for curiosity, to see the personality and the knowledge behind the postings. It is indeed astonishing what people write there and what they believe. I am truly sorry for all those honest seekers which are polluted with spiritual nonsense and I hope that God keeps care of them and protects them from too much misleading rubbish.

Recently there were again very unhealthy discussions where I want to clear some points:

From a point of wisdom, considering spiritual development and a deep understanding of divine laws, Rudolf Steiner and his school are not useful and not recommendable. If you want to study something like this then study the main books of Blavatsky and then you have a good overview about religion and esoteric traditions but also not more. In contrary to both you can study better the books of Gottfried von Purucker who was a real genius. People become

118

quickly misled by Rudolf Steiner. He had used the whole stuff from Blavatsky, added some points and pretended that spirituality is too complex for 99,99 % of people which is simply not true. Due to his complex teachings seekers think that he was a superior genius himself and no one would ever be able to understand him – but trying to do so is entertainment for them. So indeed they do just intellectual studies which do not lead anywhere. And by the way there is so much nonsense spread that I do not know if I should laugh about it or if I should feel sorry about those followers who believe it. Certainly all needs are fulfilled by creation, also those ones.

Another point is that one should never mix up Bardon´s teachings with "traditional magic" of any kind. From a higher point of view Bardon´s teachings represent the peak of knowledge and traditional magic the bottom. There are many who do not understand this difference in quality and who think that all "systems" are more or less equal. This is not the case. Bardon represents the core and the traditional schools the shell. And I bet that there was no real master of a higher degree in a traditional school but only people with some kind of experience and some kind of abilities. And with this we come to the next point. Magical development means always also mystical development and both always mean true spiritual development. There is simply no different way possible. So when someone thinks that he can develop himself in magic without having to pay respect to spirituality or mysticism then he is simply on the wrong trip. And this is quite often the problem of traditional magic, - the focus on the development of the ego instead of higher spiritual aims. I must also say that most of the traditional techniques are of a very low quality and this is also valid for their teachings. So I recommend to focus on Bardon and other high quality spiritual stuff and to go on distance to the "traditional magic".

Then there was a discussion about the differences between East and West. True knowledge can be found in Eastern and Western teachings and all teachings which are valid come from one source. Due to the history of mankind the good stuff of teachings in the West comes nearly completely from the East, from India, China, Tibet, Persia over Greece to Europe. So those who think that the West has something special and different in teachings contrary to the East are simply wrong. Indeed the Eastern initiates have sympathy for the poor standards in the West. But it is typical for the big egos of the Western World to think to be at the peak.

Another incomprehensible dull discussion was if magicians become enlightened. It is nearly an offense to have to answer such a question as it shows how poor the degree of comprehension is among the seekers and so called advanced students or "masters". There is no real master in any tradition who is not enlightened. When you reach a certain degree of spiritual refinement you become enlightened by the nature of God which merges with you, which enlightens you with divine energies, light, consciousness and powers. So at the latest you become enlightened in the tenth step of Initiation into Hermetics. Then you unite with divine qualities and powers according to the four elements. But you can also receive enlightenment in the first step due to the silence of the mind exercise. This is just a different degree or form of enlightenment.

Now we come to a really big mistake, a major mistake in magical training with major consequences. Students who do the training, the energetic exercises tend to believe that it is all a matter of the mental plane. And so they do the charging of the element energies only on the level of thinking. This is nice but it is misses the point, the sense of the exercise. The charging has to take place on the astral level and this means often hard work to densify the energies down to the astral plane where they become nearly physical. Only when you work on the astral level you are able to transform and refine your astral body and with this to increase your power, your mastership. When you work only on the mental plane you cannot get good results, anything useful for magical operations or for your progress. And this is not only true for the work with the elements and fluids in Bardon´s first book but also and especially for Bardon´s mystical training and work in his Quabbalah. When someone states that he has accomplished the Quabbalah training and nothing happens and nothing has changed in his soul then it is simply the problem that he has done all just on a mental level and not as he should do on the astral plane. And when such a person then says that the Quabbalah training of Bardon is not practical or useful then this is really misleading.

As a last point these intellectual discussions about details for example if "being" is the highest state or if you need to "think that you are" or whatever are always perfect signs that those people have made no own and real experiences by themselves, also that they never understood the theory chapters. It often seems that they are not able to think logically or to differentiate.

For me all these things have an entertaining character if at all but for beginners such things can be very confusing and misleading and this is not positive.

My recommendation is to orientate on real masters or advanced spiritual souls and on what they write and say. When you do so you can compare their statements with the statements of such discussions and this helps to differentiate truth from half-truths and pure nonsense. I also recommend to use the own brain, logic and intuition and to do good studies on your own. And at last, just look for a good place with honest seekers and good, high quality exchange.

Certainly all needs are satisfied in our world, - good ones and bad ones.

## SATANISTS AND PSYCHOPATHS

When you study psychic diseases with their symptoms you can make an interesting discovery. The leading Satanists, those who build the elite of mankind, can be defined as psychopaths or sociopaths (antisocial personality disorder). The symptoms respectively the characteristics are quite equal. You can read more about their characteristics here:

http://en.wikipedia.org/wiki/Psychopathy#Characteristics

Interesting isn´t it?! They are all simply "ill" respectively of a different nature than normal humans. So indeed the best thing would be to give them a professional treatment in a lunatic asylum (for the rest of their lives).

The only problem is that they do not believe that they could be ill. Instead they believe that they are of a superior nature.

A good joke indeed!

Ray

## Spiritual work and hypnosis

As a spiritual person you do two things: Spiritual training for yourself and spiritual work for others. For your own spiritual training the use of your subconsciousness via autosuggestion is very important. Hypnosis as a professional bundle of different techniques for trance and the work with the subconsciousness can be a great aid. Hypnosis offers also great possibilities to work with other persons. Indeed all magical, mystical, energetical and spiritual techniques or phenomena can be integrated perfectly into the use of hypnosis. For example I integrate magical techniques and my spiritual knowledge into my work as a hypnotist for coaching, clearing and healing. Further on you can use hypnosis for all magical abilities, for contact with the deceased, for meeting your spiritual guide, for working with a medium and so on. You can train and unfold your abilities in best way by using hypnosis. You can also clean and heal your personality with hypnosis so that you do not need an eternity for the refinement and balancing of your soul, your personality. Hypnosis is indeed unlimited in its application.

Imagine you undergo a hypnotic therapy/coaching education. Then you can optimize and enhance your own work with your subconsciousness and you can help others. Now imagine you and a brother/sister on the spiritual path undergo such an education. Then you can treat each other for best results in training and development. So you reduce the time and the effort in best way and you dissolve blockades which keep you from making progress.

My conclusion is that everyone on the spiritual path should undergo such an education to widen his horizon and to have a bundle of great techniques for the work with trance. Otherwise you can choose a hypnotist of your confidence and receive treatments for an optimized training of abilities and the unfolding of your personality.

I am going to offer such hypnotic treatment for training and also coaching for the unfolding of the personality in a few weeks around April 2012. I will offer also special workshops for magical knowledge and special techniques. This will be a good thing.

## ABOUT DISCUSSIONS

Today there are countless discussions in the internet with spiritual, esoteric and X versus Y topics. I want to put some light on such discussions to ease your life when you decide to take part.

At first view you might think that the topic of the discussion meets the headline, for example "creation versus evolution" and so you discuss the pro and contra. Indeed the headline topic is not the real topic and interesting only on the surface. It is similar to an iceberg. Only a small part is visible but the main part is under the surface. In the discussions the main part is the psychological field. Here we have often the same groups of people. We have a very few pioneers who work for new insights and a deeper comprehension, for truth itself. They love research and often have a scientific character or are dreamers, people with great visions. Then there are groups of believers, people who believe in their tradition, in their religion, their teachings without any idea to question them. Instead of being critical in a positive way to find truth beyond pure belief they work on justifying their opinions, their belief. This is a matter of feeling safe and of protecting their own philosophy. Then there are people who believe to be superior and who use such discussions to feed their egos by offending and fighting others. I would call them simply assholes. Certainly there are a few other groups of people in such discussions but those are the main ones. In conclusion the main aspect of such discussions is not to gain new insights but to fight against each other for protection of the own belief/philosophy and to affront others to satisfy the ego. When you understand this psychological aspect which is indeed the main topic, - subconsciously certainly, then you can cope better with such discussions. The only healthy way is to look for serious, open people who are really interested in widening the own horizon, in learning and growing together and to start with them a more or less closed research group.

A further point: Imagine the fact that you have a certain amount of information about a topic. Maybe you have made own experiences or maybe you have information from sources your trust. Three factors are important concerning information: The quantity, the quality and the congruence. In main you have a certain, limited amount of useful information about a topic where you rely on and where you build on your own belief, opinion or philosophy. This is often similar to a puzzle which is not complete, where details are missing or whole parts of the picture. So in life you meet other people and you do exchange with them about a topic. The exchange can lead to completing your puzzle, your picture of the topic or to an optimization, to changes but also to a complete reconstruction. Here is always the question how good are my information, how complete and does the other person has more or better information or is it the other way around. These questions and deliberations are always valid when you meet other people in discussions. In best case it feels easy for you to enrich and to complete your belief/knowledge and worst case you feel the need to protect your belief although it is not true. In "another" best case you know that you are right because of your good and complete information and that the other one is wrong respectively believes in half-truths but you feel no need to fight to convince him as his opinion fits his degree of maturity. In worst case you know you are right and try to convince people who are not ready and so you throw pearls to the pigs and see yourself in a dirty verbal war. So discussions are indeed a matter of information, - of completeness, quality and congruence. And it is certainly wise to listen to those who have more and better information than oneself.

A last and especially interesting aspect of such discussions is the use of the terms "science" and "scientific". People love to implicate that science means absolute truth and so that everything which is scientific must be right. But this is not true. Indeed science has replaced religion but works in main in the same way. In former times the high priests appeared omniscient and omnipotent; today they are replaced by the scientists who appear in this way. And what is called "Science" is completely based on the philosophy of materialism. Science today is not free of belief. It is also not free of ego, of money issues, of interpretation and so on. Science today is in main something relative. Only mathematics and physics are absolute. The other sciences have much to do with belief and interpretation. Beside this real science would respect all beliefs and would do research without limitations or presumptions. For example it is quite funny to observe how many strange phenomena in medicine, psychotherapy, archaeology and so on appear nearly daily, which cannot be explained by materialistic science but perfectly by a spiritual philosophy and which are suppressed officially because of these problems. If you interview scientists about strange phenomena unofficially they would tell you unbelievable stories but when you ask them officially they would deny as they fear to lose their jobs.

This is the funny, materialistic world we are living in. Materialism is the darkest invention and we pay a high price for it.

## PROBLEMS OF MANKIND AND THEIR SOLUTION

There is a very simple solution for mankind: We just have to give the elite a psychotherapeutic treatment and replace them with wise men. This would solve directly all problems. Our elite consist obviously of psychopaths and sociopaths as it is scientifically defined. Our leaders are ill, very ill and they do not know it. In contrary they believe that they are superior, enlightened and that their initiation and training in their secret societies is right and good. In fact they lose important spiritual/human characteristics respectively suppress them and pervert them. The consequences we all have to bear!

How could we prevent that sociopaths, psychopaths and other ill and dangerous people get into positions of power where they reign over people and are able to spread their poison for major damages in life and society?

The answer is quite simple and consists of two aspects: The first aspect is that it is absolutely necessary to reintegrate positive human values back into life and society, - especially in the education of the young ones. People have to orientate on these values. They have to be the guiding ideals in life, in behavior. Negative behavior must come along with damaging reputation. It can´t be accepted and society must show it. The second aspect is that we need suitability tests for all leading positions. Today there are a lot of people in positions of power who are not suitable at all. I speak here especially about the human, psychological suitability. So in fact everyone who wants to lead other people has to pass successfully a suitability test where his personality is checked, his ability to take responsibility for subordinates and his professional skills.

When we do so in all aspects of society then we will be able to restore a good and healthy form of order which provides a healthy society and balance in life.

The main problem today are indeed the destructive ill leaders with their unholy ideologies. When we are able to get rid of them then healing takes place naturally.

Ray

## Special Techniques for Target-Imagination

Bardon recommends to imagine yourself as having already reached your aim, - a new ability or a new quality for example. This idea is called today target-imagination as you start with your target/aim. In contrary there is the process-imagination which works on the process to optimize it. In best case both techniques are used in combination. This you can do as "mental training", meditation, autosuggestion or pure imagination training.

When you do target-imagination then you meditate, imagine the wished for state or ability/quality. It is somehow a form of simulation with corresponding thoughts, feelings and behavior. Certainly this works.

Besides this there is something which is more or less unknown, which provides a new perspective on the idea of target-imagination. Here the main point is to "jump" from your current state into the target-state. This is something very special and a different experience to the normal training. It is comparable with mental/astral traveling where you change your place/situation immediately. Here you travel into the wished for state. This means the wished for state does exist already and with your additional meditation/imagination work you strengthen and vitalize this state.

The act of "jumping" or traveling can be done in two simple ways. First way: Keep your meditation position and imagine your wished for state in front of you – which means you imagine yourself in front of you with the desired ability/quality. When you have done enough imagination work then imagine that your wished for personality moves into yourself sitting in meditation. Indeed you merge with your "future"-self. Something like this works already with real imagination (!) Therefore one speaks also of "information", - working with "information". The second technique is a meditation in standing position. Again you imagine your wished for state/personality in front of you. When you are ready you step into it – for examples after three steps forward you are in your new personality. In general when you have merged with your target-personality/imagination then imagine that you integrate all new energies, qualities and abilities now which can be integrated instantly and that all qualities, abilities, energies which have to develop do so automatically to unfold your target-imagination/personality. At last enjoy your new state and come back into the waking state. You can repeat such techniques certainly as you like.

Before you do such a technique I recommend to dissolve all blockades which keep you from reaching the wished for state. Do this in a meditation. If you like then work with light which floods your whole microcosm clearing your blockades and healing it automatically. Let the light enter your body at your crown chakra/ head and lead it through your whole body and out at your hands and feet. Concentrate on dissolving especially the blockades regarding your wished for state/abilities/qualities.

These techniques can be really amazing and powerful with great results. It is indeed real magic.

So enjoy it and use it for your development.

## PAST-LIFE-THERAPY: TRAVELING THROUGH SPACE & TIME

I have made a training in reincarnation therapy which was very fascinating. The point is that you as a hypnotist can induce a trance where the client is enabled to travel into a former personality in a former life and a former setting of landscape and situation like virtual reality. Everything feels absolutely real, all your senses perceive reality, a reality of a former time. You can feel the sunlight on your skin, you feel the warmth of the summer, you can smell the salt of the air at the sea, you can feel the wet grass under your feet, you can see your former body, your former cloths, your former appearance and you can perceive your former beloved ones and so on. It is unbelievable and truly a great and mind blowing experience.

Beside this you have full access to your former knowledge and your abilities. Imagine this! I have led back a client who experienced himself as a bard in old England. He was an initiate of the caste of the Druids. Guess what kind of knowledge he had! This is simply amazing. I gave him the suggestion that he is able to remember everything from this life in his present life.

Then it is certainly possible to meet your spiritual guide, your beloved ones which have died already. You can travel through space and time into all places of the astral world and everywhere in history for research.

Last but not least – through such experiences your mind becomes very flexible so that you can move on your own in former personalities, situations and lives. Mind traveling or mental traveling becomes astonishing easy.

We did also something very precious – real karma clearing. We dissolved in trance all bad karma from former life times with bad influences on the present life. Do you know what this means? Liberty!

In conclusion I can only recommend again a complete high quality education in hypnotherapy including all kinds of application and techniques. It will push you in your spiritual development. Thanks to hypnosis you will be able to unfold yourself and all abilities much easier and better than going the normal way.

Required is certainly a high quality standard in education and appliance.


## TRADITIONAL KABBALAH VERSUS BARDON´S COSMIC LANGUAGE

Hello D.,

first of all let me say that I respect all religions and spiritual traditions. So I am certainly not against tradition.

Regarding Bardon and "traditions" we have a general "difference" throughout all of his teachings. Bardon is not teaching from a traditional background. Bardon teaches from the opposite point. This means he was dedicated to present universal teachings independent from time, religion and culture. These universal teachings are certainly reflected in all spiritual traditions and religions. His wish was to present universal teachings which spiritual seekers from all kinds of belief can integrate into their own background (as far as necessary).

Regarding KTQ - it is older than the Jewish tradition, it is the universal creative language of God. So indeed it is independent from any traditions. And so there is no need to bind it to a language or tradition. It is just a matter of situation that Bardon has grown up in Middle Europe so that he has used the Roman alphabet. Important are only the tones - not the language.

Certainly Bardon refers to the Sefer Yetzirah as it is one of the latest and known documents which talks about the cosmic language. But he does not say that one has to study it. Somewhere in his theory part in KTQ he says that today there is no need to learn Jewish to be able to learn the practical Quabbalah and obviously he is right. So he differentiates between Jewish tradition/language and the universal cosmic language. Certainly he does not "prohibit" the studies of traditional teachings but there is no need to do so and the main point is the practical training of the pure universal system. When you try to bind the universal teachings to the Jewish tradition then you will have several problems as it is not completely compatible and it will be a try to limit something universal to time and culture.

In short words: If you do the training with KTQ then you will receive more than you can think of and you won´t find any need for tradition or something else as there is nothing beyond.

By the way: R. has spend much time to mix KTQ with the Jewish teachings. The big question is: Has this work provided any bigger results than practical training of KTQ itself?

From my experiences you have the choice if you want to take the traditional Jewish path of Kabbalah with its results or if you want to take the universal path with KTQ. Certainly it is up to you.

## CIRCLE TECHNIQUE FOR DISSOCIATION

In magic we use circles to show and to manifest the unity with God. When we stand in the center of a magical drawn circle we are one with God and no being, no force can go against us. The circle is normally used for evocation practice. But it can be used also for meditation about unity. A third use is for dissociation. In normal life human beings are connected to their beloved ones but also to those which they are in conflict with. These energetic connections are highways of emotions, of influences and they can work like chains or strings of puppet masters. Such influences – also well-meant ones – can disturb our self-determination to a sensitive point. Feeling as being not your own master in life but being a slave, puppet or living in chains is not nice. Sometimes people can be so close that you are not able to differentiate between you and the other one. In the life of a healer or a magician it is possible that there appear parasites or negative beings or deceased ones which connect to you. And there exists a variety of different influences which you maybe do not like. For all these cases where you want to get back your sovereignty, your self-determination you can use the following technique: Get into a state of trance/meditation and draw a magical circle around you. You can do it in a standing position but also in a sitting position. If you have a magical dagger/sword you can use it. If not use your imagination and the idea of unity with God. Imagine that God is drawing the circle using you as his temple.

While you do it focus on the unity and the idea that no one is allowed to disturb this holy unity, this circle. You will probably feel already the energetic connections between you and the other person/being. You can cut them with your sword or ritualistic with your imagination using a knife or scissors. Imagine them as energy channels. Now focus on the other person/being and draw a circle around him/it. Imagine that this person/being is on distance to you – no overlapping or touching circles! In this way you show that both of you are two separate beings. Cut off all negative connections between you both. Imagine that your circle blocks all bad influences and so you keep your sovereignty from now on. Finish your meditation and thank God for divine support in this matter. Whatever the reason might be for all the influences and problems – it is possible that you have to repeat this ritual for a few times. It is also possible that you discover further connections to other people/beings. Further on it can be useful to create energetic shields against attacks or attempts to influence you. In conclusion it makes much sense to "say" with drawing a circle "this is me, my personality and the other circle is you, not me". It is good to differentiate between yourself, what belongs to yourself and other ones and the things which do not belong to you.

## GAMES FOR TRAINING

At the moment I am working overtime which costs much energy. In short breaks I play a small game called Bengal which trains the speed of reaction. Meanwhile I am really fast and have a good overview to react in the right way. Thinking about such small games it came into my mind that those games could be created for magical training, for example of imagination skills. You start with something really easy and with each step you increase your abilities until you reach mastership. In form of a game training makes fun and can be done also in breaks at work or normal spare time. I think that in the future such games will be a standard for all kinds of skills, normal ones and especially paranormal ones, magical ones. If God is kind to me I will push the development of such games in the future.

## AIR ELEMENT FOR REGENERATION

Imagine you have stress, you feel exhausted or somehow imbalanced. If this is the case then you can help yourself in a good and easy way: When you go to bed then charge your sleeping room with air element and keep it there over the night. So you will sleep in an atmosphere of air element and this will be good for your lungs, your heart chakra, your immune system and all functions which are connected to the air element. A supply of much air element over night means that your body increases all balancing processes, - clearing, healing and harmonizing. So you will regenerate on all three planes in a good way. Further on it is possible that you will make experiences with mental traveling as the air element can make your mental body loose. Also you can experience high feelings, a good sleep, peace, vastness, a higher form of love.

Just try it and do it for 1-3 nights for good effects.

## THE UNIVERSAL SOLVENT AND REMEDY CALLED LOVE

Certainly I have written already about love as a great remedy but I want to focus again on it as we human beings tend to forget about important things. Love has many aspects. Here I want to discuss only the energetic ones. From the perspective of a Quabbalist there exist already a variety of letters which have different qualities/powers and which belong all to love. These are divine qualities which do not really deal with human matters. As human beings we can experience that the expression of love towards a person or an animal has a solvent effect and a connecting, uniting effect. This means when we express feelings of love to another being we dissolve automatically all kinds of boundaries between each other, also resistance and an eventual hostile attitude will be dissolved, melted down. An opening takes place, a bridge is built and a form of unity manifests. There is a rapport, a harmony between two individuals. It is an integrating process, a floating unity.

As we see love causes good effects naturally between people in love. Expressing love has everywhere a healing effect as negative attitudes/energies are melted and a higher unity is built. In such a unity no hurting can take place. This is important to understand. Therefore love means also peace, health and security. It means further on freedom, respect and self-determination, it means acceptance and positive interdependence. It has many positive meanings.

So you can show love to other people, to animals, plants, then to God, to higher beings and at last to all beings in creation. When you face people with a negative attitude with love then they have problems to act against you, to hurt you. They simply are not able to get into resonance with you, to connect to you. (Depending on the degree of being negative it can mean that you have to express much love, a strong radiance of love.)

You can also charge your rooms with love or a landscape, a city, the whole planet. Where you charge love, love will unfold its power of healing and cleaning, of harmony and peace. In old India the initiates blessed at least their whole village or area with love and enlightening energies to keep up peace and good social care. You can do similar things.

And now I want to come to my main topic. You can and should use the power of love to heal yourself, to balance yourself and to clear yourself from bad karma, from bad qualities, from bad attitudes and habits. Love has also transforming powers. With love you can transform bad characteristics into good ones. With love you can integrate what is missing.

For practice it is good to charge the whole microcosm with love and to meditate step by step about the clearing, healing and integration of all aspects of your personality regarding your whole body with all regions and all organs, on all planes. This is similar to the descriptions of Bardon regarding the work with vital energy charging the whole body, all regions and all organs. Charge also your aura and work on it in the same way. Imagine that you are in the center of pure love and there is nothing but love. And don´t forget to send love into your chakras and into your nadis (energy channels) so that love is floating through your whole energetic system to clear, heal and balance it. It is possible that you feel a higher activity or pain or bad emotions in an organ, region or chakra. If so then work intensively on it. In general meditate that the love dissolves also your bad karma, all bad energies from former life times. Clear and heal yourself from the dirt of your past and your past lives. This means liberty. You can repeat this meditation/work several times until you have a clear feeling that you are completely healed. Such a work can accelerate your spiritual development very much and it can make your life blossom.

In general – if you are confronted with something negative: Send love to it! And if you need peace and security then charge yourself with love.

Last point: On earth there live really big assholes, psychopaths, ill people and certainly also normal negative people. Then there are many people with problems, with big challenges to master. If you want to do something useful then you can bless them with love. Although they won´t say "Thank you" you do something really good for them, for their souls. And what you do for them returns to yourself. "Heal and be healed!" Remember Karma Yoga?

Love is omnipotent. Don´t forget this!

We all need healing.


## ABOUT PAST-LIFE-THERAPY

Just a few words: What are we human beings at last? We are the sum of all experiences and processes of growing from all our past lives. This is true for all our positive characteristics and also for all our negative qualities. In the so called past life therapy all former incarnations can be experienced and examined. The aim is to discover the causes which are responsible for problems in your present life. As soon as you become aware of a situation in the past which caused your present problems you are able to get rid of them and this quite easy. On the other hand you can discover the causes for abilities, talents, good characteristics, interests and so on, also the causes for relationships today. And if you want you can travel also back into the times between two incarnations, your stay in the astral realms. Depending on the used technique you can meet your spiritual guide, spiritual masters and you can communicate with your personal god, your divine self. So you get all information and explanations you need or want to receive.

In conclusion past life therapy is a very precious tool for the spiritual development, for healing, for liberation, for dissolving bad karma and for raising your awareness. I recommend every spiritual seeker to do research on his past lives with hypnosis. Look for a good hypnotist and clear at least your main problems with his help.

## THE PERSONAL GOD

In "Memories of Franz Bardon" Dr. M. K. talks in a very few sentences about having to choose the qualities of his personal god during a car ride with his master Franz Bardon. That´s all we get to know about the "personal god". I want to put some more light on this topic for a better understanding and practical use. As you know the human being corresponds with the macrocosm with its different spheres, powers and qualities. So the human being is composed of different planes, powers and qualities like the macrocosm. Behind the diversity there is the all permeating unity. As you also know on the planes of mind and divine spirit time and space are not really existent. In sum this all means that beside the relative personality of a human being which represents an incarnation and a step of spiritual development, there is also the perfect divine and absolute being which is beyond time and space. It is the divine self which is guiding the relative human being/personality through the countless incarnations and which is waiting for the mystical wedding, the unfolding of the divine nature in the human temple, the reconnection, the unity of God and human being. Indeed when we undergo a spiritual training we refine ourselves to a degree that our personal god can connect to us and in later steps can be integrated more and more in our nature, personality. This is the aim of the first Tarot Card. In the third Tarot Card we connect and integrate the macrocosmic God, the divine nature in its highest powers and virtues. But back to the topic. So for practical application we can think of the personal god as the divine model of ourselves, as a real divine being which is you in perfection and which you can connect and talk to as your personal god is omniscient and can answer your questions. So in a state of trance, in meditation you can call on your personal god to speak with him/her. You can also meditate about merging with your personal god to take part in his nature to refine yourself. Bardon makes only a few comments about these things. All have the same direction – to give your god a form. I recommend to imagine your god looking like you but in divine perfection, golden, expressing divine virtues (love, wisdom, power, etc.). When you do a meditation about his/her appearance you will probably get useful insights and visions for a good imagination/form. You can cooperate with your personal god in all magical tasks, for healing, for insights in your past lives, for a lot of good things. It is a wonderful experience to meet your personal god and to work with him/her.

By the way – the term "higher self" means the personal god but the term and its use is not well chosen respectively quite limited. Personal god or divine self are better.

Enjoy the experience of your divinity!

## HEALING AND KARMA

Just short: Regarding healing work we can differentiate between two kinds of diseases, symptoms and problems in general. One type can and should be healed, is indeed waiting for healing. The other type does not want to be healed as it has a deeper sense. The first type is similar to dirt or rubbish which remains just because no one is there to clean it. So if you as a healer clear it then it is vanished and no longer a problem. Just as simple. It is a matter of psychic, karmic hygiene. It is certainly also a matter of useful, good behavior of the concerned person. As you clean up your rooms and make them look better from time to time you should do the same with your personality and the world you are living in. Back to the second type. Here the problem, disease or symptoms are a necessary wished for lesson to learn. So indeed the problem provides the chance to collect necessary, important experiences to grow in personality, to make a further step in the spiritual development of the soul. Many lessons are certainly not funny, not pleasant but often hard to bear. The only thing a healer can do here is to help the patient to get a deeper insight about his symptoms. A good technique is to use hypnosis to let the patient talk to his spiritual guide or personal god to be informed about the causes for his problems. It is also possible to show the patient like a movie the situations in the past which led to this lesson. Further on you can also let the patient experience with all senses the causing situation. But these details are left to the individual situation. You can also create a room for insights about his problem (without spiritual guide, etc.). Such deeper insights in his karma, in his lesson to learn and his problems can bring much relief to the patient. Then he is able to cope better with his hard fate. And one should not forget that it was his own decision to make these hard experiences! Certainly he did so in a higher state of consciousness.

In conclusion healers should clear and balance completely the first type, the rubbish of the soul which no one has cleaned before. And the second type has to be respected and in best way the patient should become aware of it. Then you have made a good job. If it should be not directly clear what the lesson is respectively which symptoms belong to it then ask the spiritual leader of the patient or his divine self for guidance and help. Both are very cooperative. Again I recommend to learn hypnosis, hypnotherapy and past-life therapy. Then there will be nothing what you cannot treat successfully. Here you can also work perfectly with magic and energetic healing as you can combine such techniques very good.

## THE CHALICE OF FORGIVENESS

A nice technique: Imagine a wonderful golden chalice, if you like with gems on it. Imagine that this is the chalice of love, forgiveness and healing. Imagine that it has the power to dissolve bad karma, that it heals on all three planes, that it is a chalice which is always full. And now imagine that you take this chalice and drink the water of life, love, forgiveness and healing. Drink as much as you can. Drink as long as you need to be filled with these waters of life, of forgiveness. Remember that you can drink as much as you like because it is energy which fills your soul (not like normal water filling your stomach). Imagine that this water fills you with love, with forgiveness for all your "sins", that it heals you deeply. Heal yourself with the chalice of forgiveness.

And as you can heal yourself you can heal others as well. Give those who need love, forgiveness and healing the chalice in your imagination and let them drink a lot until they feel healed and satisfied. In this way you can do a lot of good.

As there exists a chalice of forgiveness there also exists a pool of forgiveness, love and healing. Imagine a wonderful pool looking like those of the former times for kings and queens. Imagine that this pool is filled with the water of life, of forgiveness, love and healing. And now jump into it and enjoy! The pool is big enough so that you can invite/imagine also others who are in need for love, forgiveness and healing bathing in the pool. It is a great experience.

And last but not least you can repeat such good things as often as you like and need.

## DISEASES OF THE PRESENT LIFE

Regarding medicine and healing treatments: We experience in the present incarnation all kinds of diseases, symptoms, problems, injuries, etc. Then we have the perception that these things are phenomena of this life and we are going to treat them – causes and effects - only regarding this life. This approach is comprehensible but not holistic. Research with hypnosis and past life therapy has shown that for all and I repeat it for all diseases, injuries and so on in this life there are karma seeds, causes in one or more past lives. This is very important to understand. This is also true for so called genetic diseases. And here we have to differentiate again between old rubbish of the soul which can be cleared and healed and diseases, problems which work as lessons for important experiences to make.

In conclusion the most intelligent thing you can do is to clear your past life karma, your karma seeds as early as possible to suffer not more in this life than absolutely necessary. And second – when you do so, your future children will be really thankful as you save them the problems you have brought with you. Then if you have children work on them quite early to clear them from all bad karma seeds from their own past so that they can develop as good as possible. It is all a matter of health and liberation. Certainly a good time before you decide to make children clear yourself and your wife from bad karma seeds. So you won´t pass on bad things.

But also know that you change with this your life and maybe the soul constellation of your family. Clearing and healing is a good thing and we all need it very much. The world needs it.

## HEALING OF THE DECEASED

At least there are two good reasons to give deceased souls healing treatments. The first one is that someone you have loved is gone and because of this positive connection you want to give him healing. The second one is that you want to clear and to heal all your karmic entanglements (which you know) regarding your family and friends. On the energetic level we have a phenomenon of inheritance where mental and emotional contents are passed on to family members of the next generation. This is a matter of energetic influence and strong relations, connections. The energetic atmosphere where you grow up has much influence on you. It is a different question how much and in which quality is passed on. This depends on your own personality. Let´s take a look at an example to understand it better. Imagine that your grandfather has experienced bad times of war and destruction. This trauma has left bad energies in his personality, maybe fears, special patterns of behavior etc. Imagine that your second grandfather had big problems with his health, maybe problems with his kidneys. Imagine that these things are not the only problems in your family. So and you are a daughter or son in the second generation and you notice strange problems in your own personality where you do not know where they come from. Let´s imagine that you do good research and discover that some things have causes in past lives and that you have received bad contents from your family, your grandfathers, etc. When you know this then you can clear, heal yourself, then your family to clear the bad influences and as your grandparents are already gone but still exist on the astral plane you can clear and heal them to dissolve all bad influences, all bad karmic connections you have with/from them. So the important point is that you should not examine yourself as an independent individual but to see yourself as a part of a system. When you want to heal this part then in fact you have to heal the whole system with all its components. So complete healing for yourself means to heal your family, also the deceased ones. You can be sure that they will be very happy when they receive healing treatments.

One simple technique is to invite them all to take a bath in the pool of forgiveness, love and healing. Just imagine them all splashing in this pool and enjoying the great healing of mind and soul. See how they release their pains, how their wounds heal, how their health and vitality is restored. See how thankful they are for the forgiveness they receive. It should be clear that you charge your imagination with all these good feelings (astral plane). This will be a really good healing treatment for them.

In the same way you can bath all living family members, friends, colleagues and so on. And you can also bath all your enemies and those who behave in a bad way regarding you. Put them all into such a pool of love, forgiveness and healing.

This is good karma yoga. And it will heal you. Remember – heal the system and you get healed.


## BALANCING OF AIR AND EARTH

This is a topic which everyone experiences in his development. The more you refine yourself the more you activate your mental/astral life. Your awareness and perception shifts from the physical world to the higher, spiritual realms. Bardon says that your interest in the physical world decreases as you live more and more on the higher realms while you are incarnated. To understand it better imagine a child with a small helium balloon. The balance is given. Now imagine that the balloon is growing and growing. The child is hardly able to withstand the lifting power of the balloon. It is short before flying away. This is the air element or principle of the air. The same happens in your spiritual development – you grow and grow and you are short before flying away. It can feel hard to keep down on earth as your weight is reduced to nearly nothing and the sky (astral realms) is your true home. So what can you do to be more down here in the physical world? You must increase your weight – with the earth element. Charging with the earth element helps to get your feet back on the ground. It is a real balancing effect between air and earth. The work with the earth element is also a possibility to "make holidays from God" which means that you feel more human and less connected. It is a mystery of the earth element and the quabbalistic letter AE (Ä).

Just remember that you can balance too much air/feeling too airy with earth element. Sometimes this can be quite useful.

## THREE MAIN ASPECTS OF HEALING

Why do we need healing at all? Something happens in life which causes an imbalance in your personality. Imbalance means that something is out of order, that something does not work as it should. Energetically it means that there are energies now in the system which are ill, exhausted, bad, unhealthy.

The first aspect of healing is cleaning. You have to get rid of the bad, ill energies. The second aspect is to restore the order, to restore health, harmony. And the third aspect is to become aware of the circumstances which caused the imbalance. These are the three main aspects of healing. It is important to understand this when you work as a healer. It sounds quite banal but it isn´t. If you want to restore health without cleaning it won´t really work. If you want to clean the patient without restoring the harmony/health then it is like keeping wounds open. If you want to heal without making the patient aware of the causes then the patient can get the same problems again easily.

When you take a look at the different healing techniques then you can discover that they often set a different focus regarding these three aspects. The results are corresponding to it.

Absolutely necessary is the cleaning aspect. Healing can take place by itself but certainly it is better to support this process. The third aspect, the raising of the awareness is "good to have" but not absolutely necessary. It is especially useful and important for spiritual seekers as they want to refine and increase their consciousness. The increasing of the awareness itself is often already the major step for healing. Certainly in best case you support all three aspects of healing.

## MIND PROGRAMMING

When we examine the human nature we discover a phenomenon which can be described as programs, programming and patterns of thoughts, emotions and behavior. In a certain situation we make a certain experience. This experience causes an insight with corresponding thoughts in our mind. These thoughts cause corresponding feelings or emotions. The whole experience with thoughts and emotions causes a corresponding behavior. We have learned something and we record it as a program, pattern for similar situations or to avoid such situations in the future. Here we can differentiate between good situations, normal ones (neutral) and bad ones. Good situations we enjoy and we program to re-experience them. Normal situations are for everyday use and we program them just as a useful ability/behavior like using cars, etc. Bad situations lead to a program of avoiding them. It means to change the behavior, to reprogram to never get into such a situation again.

The programming develops the maximum effectiveness in an exceptional intensive situation. If something small happens you do not mind. If something big happens you are really excited and the programming effect is big and lasting. Imagine you feel the heat of a fire. Your experience is "Okay, fire is hot, I should keep distance." Imagine now you fall into a fire and you burn yourself. Then your experience is traumatic "I will never get near to a fire. Fire is evil." So in the first case you have no problem with fire. In the second one you have changed your behavior to avoid such a situation in the future. The point here is that the behavior does not change to a realistic, adequate degree - a careful handling of fire, but to an extreme pattern of behavior, here in this example the total avoidance of any kind of fire. This extreme pattern leads to problems for the concerned person and limits him in his life. Fire is just an example. When you think about all the fears which exist and how they limit people in their behavior. The problem is always the extreme behavior, pattern, the program.

In normal life there are already enough situations where you learn and program yourself in good and negative ways. But there are also these exceptional intensive situations which have a lasting effect for a life time or more. They can happen in the life and often life also ends in such a situation. Imagine someone is going to die in the next minutes or hours. He reaches a special state of clarity where he gets important insights about his life, his failures, problems, etc. In such a situation an insight can unfold an effect, a program which controls the next incarnation. Imagine what this means. An extreme idea, program controls many years or the whole life in your next incarnation. Imagine for example you were a rich man and short before your death you have the insight that all your wealth was a matter of exploitation of poor people. This insight leads to the program "I will never be rich again!" And now imagine you are born again and you experience that you are not able to be successful in your business, that you earn only as much as absolutely necessary for your survival. And you ask yourself why you are not able to make any progress. You cannot understand it. So in fact it is just the extreme and negative program which keeps you suffering. Until this program is not removed and changed to an adequate program you will suffer.

When we take a look at the fates of people then we can discover that this kind of extreme programming is the cause for a lot of long-lasting problems without obvious reasons.

Another kind of programming are all kinds of religious and spiritual vows and promises. When you are a monk and make a vow for poverty, altruistic service and sexual abstinence then you will have big problems in the next incarnation with making money and finding a wife.

In conclusion it is very important to get insights about your own programs, to delete the negative, extreme ones and to reprogram yourself for a positive thinking, feeling and behavior. Meditation is useful and also hypnosis techniques of regression and past life therapy.

And beside these programs - the topic of being/feeling guilty together with forgiveness and healing through unconditioned love are most important in life. Discover where and why you feel guilty. Then bless you and all concerned people with love and forgiveness. And let yourself and the others receive a deep healing by the power of divine love.

## BREATHING EXERCISE

During the day it is possible that your performance goes down, that you feel tired, exhausted. Maybe you have headaches or you can´t focus on your work. It is possible that you work just too much. Maybe the air of your rooms is bad as you do not ventilate enough. For all cases you can do a short breathing exercise which helps very good. Go out into the fresh air or at least go to a window and open it. Then stand with your legs close to another and your arms at your sides. Now when you inhale then lift up your arms to the height of your shoulders and when you exhale let them go down to your sides. Breathe in a natural, slow way and deep into your belly. Inhale through your nose and exhale through your mouth. Fill your lungs completely. Keep the air for a moment and then exhale slowly. Repeat this several times until you feel better. The lateral lifting of your arms while inhaling supports the act of breathing. It makes it easier to fill your lungs. You can enhance this exercise by imagining that you inhale from all sides vital energy into your body and that you exhale wasted energies, headaches, etc. – both certainly in combination with the normal breathing of air.

The conscious breathing increases your level of oxygen and releases too much carbon dioxide. This increases naturally your performance and you feel better. Air and air element have a balancing effect on the human being. The vital energy supports your whole performance additionally.

If you like you can shake out your whole physical body so that the energy flow is optimized. Tapping the whole surface of your body is also quite healthy.

You can use this exercise also for getting up in the morning, after meditation, sports, work and any time you feel the need to increase your level of energy.

## ADDITION FOR INTROSPECTION

Bardon suggests to make the soul mirrors for the good and bad qualities of your character regarding the four elements. This is a very important work which fits perfectly in Bardon's system of spiritual development. From a psychological point of view you can and should widen the introspective work. When you follow Bardon you receive a very good overview about your character with which you can work on your refinement. Additionally you should become aware of your personal values, your idols, your needs, your wishes and aims for life and your motives, your motivation. So this is already a good amount of work and meditation. The next point is to question all you have discovered about yourself. Question your motives, your aims and so on. Become aware why you have them and what you expect to gain or to have when you realize them. Try to find out where all these things come from and where they lead to. As a result you increase your awareness about yourself, the things which move you and the things you long for. And you will think about if you want to keep everything as it is or if you want to correct or add something. All these things you can discuss with your spiritual guide in meditation/trance or under hypnosis. He can give you further information but you can also do research on your own to understand your problems/values/aims. It makes sense to think about these things from time to time as life is a process of changes. The whole topic is a matter of orientation. Where am I? Where do I come from? Where do I go? Orientation is very important in life.

## INDIRECT HEALING TECHNIQUE

I have talked about healing already really much. I just want to add two points. For your own healing which includes manifesting also harmony in your life and your relationships the following technique is very useful: Imagine the earth in the size of a ball in front of you. Now imagine that the earth has a mental and also an astral plane and a radiance, aura, all like a human microcosm. Now imagine to charge the "microcosm", the sphere of the earth on the higher planes with divine love, that this love permeates the earth and its aura. Imagine that this love blesses the earth with all its beings including mankind, etc. with forgiveness, deep healing and enlightenment. For the love quality you can use a pink color and for the enlightenment a white color. While you charge and bless the earth with all beings and mankind you should think and feel "Love for all, forgiveness for all, healing for all and enlightenment for all!" I personally like to do it this way but you can also use your hands and your crown and heart chakra to bless the earth in front of you. The whole technique can be certainly individualized. Important are just love, forgiveness, healing and enlightenment.

So what happens when you bless the earth, mankind and all beings with thoughts and feelings of love, forgiveness, healing and enlightenment? It changes your relationship to earth, mankind and all beings. You will be perceived as a good, spiritual being, maybe as an ambassador of God. A healing of your relationships takes place, you will receive support from creation and you will heal yourself. Give love and you will receive love. Just as simple. Although you might not directly change everything on earth you still do something of value. It is something good and it is something you can do daily. I recommend this practice for many positive purposes.

So, second point: I have already written about meeting with your spiritual guide. You can ask your guide to meet you in an imagined temple or in a white room or on a meadow or wherever you feel it is good. And then you can beg him/her to heal you, to inspire you for successful healing, for learning your lesson. And probably your spiritual guide is so kind to help you.

You know, sometime or maybe often the problem lies in details. When you pray for healing in general then it is possible that no one feels directly addressed to react. When you pray for healing speaking directly to your spiritual guide or healing angels or a special being then the reaction can be much better. So in general it can be very important to think deeply about the right formulation.

And in general – just try things, just do it and examine the results. Don´t get trapped in too much intellectual thinking.

## The Development of the Self-Awareness

To become aware of yourself, of who you are, what you are, also in relation/comparison to creation and God is a main point in the spiritual development. The normal human self-awareness, knowledge about oneself is quite limited. It is limited to your name, some of your characteristics, what you like and what not, your appearance, etc. This normal self-consciousness can be increased, changed or reduced more or less easy. It often depends on the success in life, on how other people perceive oneself. If you get compliments or get insulted.

In contrary the spiritual self-awareness is in a process of growing, of refinement and of crystallization. The more you make progress in your training, in your spiritual development, the more your consciousness and self-awareness transform to a brilliant, - clear, with facets, unbreakable like a diamond, showing all colors in perfect beauty. Indeed it is getting more and more absolute, untouchable, perfect. When you know who you are, when you know yourself then nothing can disturb your consciousness. It is all a matter of self-knowledge. It is very positive and lets you manage your challenges in life in a better, stronger way. At last your whole being becomes like a brilliant.

## THE TRUE PROBLEM OF MANKIND

Throughout the centuries people have been thinking about the reason for all the problems mankind has permanently to face. Some said that people lack of the spiritual knowledge of unity in diversity. Other said that we lack of wisdom, the handling of the divine-natural laws of creation. Then there are wise men who say that the earth is a school and that we are here to make experiences, good ones and bad ones. Others say that we just lack of unconditional love, of divine love.

I say that all are true. The primary problem is a little bit different. The primary problem is that we lack of light, that we lack of spiritual sunlight. To understand this better imagine a flower which grows only at a place in direct sunlight near the equator where it is warm, sunny all the year with good air and good rain. These are optimal conditions for a good development. So the flower grows rapidly to big seize in best health, etc. Now imagine the same flower somewhere in the North where it is cold, where the sun shines only temporarily, where the sky is often clouded with too much rain. Guess how the flower will grow under these bad conditions. If it survives it will grow only a little bit and does not develop many blossoms. It will be in an unhealthy condition. It cannot unfold its nature as it is possible under optimal conditions like at the equator.

Let's take this metaphor for mankind. We simply miss the divine sunlight which lets us grow under best conditions, which lets us unfold our true nature in best way. Indeed we are lost somewhere in a dark place with not much light at all. Instead of the spiritual sunlight we are fed by the artificial light of money, consumption, might, media, crime, sex, drugs and so on. The elite says that we do not need sunlight, that artificial light is better and fulfills all needs and wishes. But in fact we degenerate, get ill and die from this too much of artificial light and the too little of real sunlight. In dark places only bad things are able to grow. And so we suffer and work hard, very hard to grow so much that we are able to see the sun, to receive the divine sunlight to nourish mind and soul.

It is the problem of the fall of mankind into matter. Once mankind enjoyed living in the divine atmosphere where everything and everyone was naturally enlightened. But one day the separation started and mankind sunk into the density of the material world where the spiritual realms got disconnected, unreachable for most humans.

In the same way the solution is possible, necessary. As soon as the spiritual realms are reconnected to our world, as soon as the spiritual atmosphere is restored mankind will live in love, wisdom and peace. People hope for this time to come where the sun sphere spreads much more light down to our realms.

Beside this major problem mankind faces a second one, - the ability to keep the light. This is a matter of structure. When your energetic structure is so refined and crystallized that you can receive and keep the spiritual light then it doesn't matter where you are as you will be always connected to the divine sunlight and you will always receive it. This is an important topic of the spiritual development – to refine and crystallize your structure to receive and keep the divine energies forever.

It is indeed so important to grow beyond the darkness to receive the light and to grow strong to be able to keep it.

May God be kind to bless us all with spiritual energies so that we can grow as it is foreseen for us.

## THE MYSTERY OF FULLNESS

Do you know the differences between light and darkness? Light is something and darkness is nothing. Light is positive and darkness is negative. Light means fullness, abundance, completeness. Darkness means emptiness, nothingness.

Imagine a room which is dark as there is no light in it. And now imagine that someone turns on the light and the darkness has vanished immediately. Where light is there can't be darkness. Where fullness is there can't be emptiness. Where life is can't be death. Where love is can't be hate. And so on. This means we should replace all negative qualities by their positive opposites to become complete, full, to become a part of the natural-divine abundance which is the principle of creation.

When you meditate about this natural-divine abundance, when you set yourself into it and when you take part in this flow of energy, of abundance for all creatures in creation then you will notice that abundance has a lot of aspects like being complete, being in the right place of the natural-divine order, being okay, being appreciated, being loved, being happy, satisfied, successful, guided and so on. And you will notice that when you incorporate fullness that there is no place for fears, for sadness, for doubts, for deficiency in anything.

So set yourself into the natural-divine abundance, be abundance, think abundance, feel abundance, act as a channel of and for abundance in creation, be light, get rid of darkness. Live the principle of fullness!


## ABOUT PARAPSYCHOLOGY

Parapsychology is for spiritual people and for magicians in big parts pure torture as it is built on the materialistic belief and ignores the inner teachings of the spiritual traditions. In contrary parapsychology constructs funny to strange theories about special psi-powers and the function of "paranormal" perception. Although these aspects are real torture to read it also has positive useful aspects. The parapsychologist Milan Ryzl for example has made good research why what happens successfully, how (on the surface) spiritual people produce paranormal things and so on. So indeed there are useful information and hints in the work of parapsychologists for the own training of magical abilities. Although Ryzl was a famous and worldwide known expert, professor for parapsychology he lacked of so much knowledge and had such a limited comprehension together with misunderstandings and wrong conclusions that it is amazing. On the other hand he provided good work from the materialistic point of view. If you compare his work with Bardon´s explanations then it is the same like comparing a mud hut with a modern skyscraper. But I don´t want to criticize Ryzl. He did the best he could do. My conclusion is to read one or two books about parapsychological research and to use what is useful for experiments and training. I must say that such books often contain better information than so called "magical books". It is also possible to take part in parapsychological workshops. I did it as a part of my hypnosis education. Some techniques and stories were really interesting but the normal parapsychological experiments with influencing playing at dice were quite boring.

## THE MATERIALISTIC DIMWITS - IGNORANT, ARROGANT AND UGLY

Bardon spoke about the materialistic belief in a very kind way. He said that the materialists worship God in his materialistic appearance, in his unlimited, powerful and beautiful manifestation as the dense material world. Certainly he is right regarding the best type of materialist. I certainly can understand people when they say that they are not able to believe things beyond their direct perception. It is simply a lack of capability to think and feel a little bit above the lowest degree. The saying "I believe only what I can see/perceive directly." Is one of the most stupid sayings of the last decades. Indeed there are countless things we cannot perceive directly but where we know that they exist and so it is no logical or useful argument. It is just very dull. A lot of energetic, electrical phenomena can´t be perceived as our senses are too limited. But we know that they exist because our physical instruments tell so. In the same way you could say that thoughts and feelings do not exist as you cannot see or hear them. So the saying is pure nonsense but very famous for idiots to proclaim proudly.

I know good materialists with much heart, best intentions and high ideals. But they are the exception. Certainly I respect the different kinds of belief as it is a matter of maturity and free will. What I do not like and which is abhorrent for me is the (s)crap of the materialists, the rejects of mankind. I must say that I show much more respect to the Satanists than to them. Every time I read about them it makes me feel sick. I write this article not to talk about my cordial dislikes but to show where they have gone wrong, where the problem is.

Throughout all centuries of the history of mankind every new generation has learned from the experiences of the older ones. It is a very simple and natural behavior, a matter of respecting the experiences which were made, of the knowledge which was gained and the wisdom of the older generation, the wisdom of life. When you want to learn a craft or an art then you go to an experienced master to learn from him. When you have finished your education you become a master one day yourself and certainly you will enrich your abilities and techniques by your own experiences. So indeed it is a process of improvement and of adaptation to new requirements and changes. And certainly it is also possible that new things occur and old things vanish. But all in all it is a continuing process of development and passing on of knowledge and techniques from one generation to the next one.

These positive and natural processes were kept by through the whole history of mankind and we often call them tradition or traditional. I mean this in a positive way. With such traditions human ideals, human values and the spiritual ideas of God, responsibility, altruistic care for the poor, karma etc. were handed on. These things have been always the basis for a working society. And everyone has known it.

Then the great disaster has happened. The materialism came up with its darkness, dullness, being godless, inhuman, unspiritual. The natural and good connection to our inheritance, to our traditions and values, to our roots was broken. It was in fact the second fall of mankind. In the first fall mankind has entered the material world still having a spiritual background and now in the second fall mankind got completely trapped in matter, in materialism and darkness. To cut off your connection to your roots, your origins is the worst thing you can do. It means to lose everything, to lose the source of life.

What happened? The leaders of people especially in the West but certainly also in communistic countries cut off all connections to their human history, to their life-giving roots. With one sweeping blow they destroyed everything and spit in the faces of their ancestors. They proclaimed that mankind was dull, bad and poor before they entered the stage. They proclaimed that they were the bearer of truth and knowledge and that they were foreseen to "heal" people from their beliefs and traditions. The results you know from communism and brutal capitalism. There was no spirit left in the souls of the people but darkness and the desire for money and consumption. As you know money and materialistic consumption cannot satisfy mind and soul.

This cutting off and the denying of the roots and all the human experiences led to a disastrous form of science, the materialistic, atheistic science built on money issues and economics interests. And here we find the dimwits, the ignorant, arrogant and ugly wiseacres. They love to proclaim that they can prove that they know nothing in many scientific fields because of their materialistic limitations and their stupid idea to believe only what they can see. They love to ignore everything which could disturb their limited philosophy and they do not perceive that their form of science is not real just because it is limited to the materialistic belief which is not proved as a universal truth. And because they ignore all former and traditional teachings, all experiences of mankind they love to develop own artificial and stupid theories about the world. And because they are slaves of money and economic, political interests they proclaim bad ideas and predictions to the people to make them anxious, to keep control and to make them pay. They are the naive servants of evil. If they have asked their ancestors what is real science about they would know that is about responsibility, truth, service, ethics with a selfless attitude. It is a sign of enormous arrogance to ignore all experiences of mankind and its history, to make the cut and to start as a dull one to create an own building of knowledge made from opinions and interests. Imagine someone who says to a professor at the university "Keep your knowledge for yourself as you are misled and a poor idiot. I know everything much better although I have never studied your knowledge. I show you the right teachings. I show you true knowledge. You are nothing. I am everything." Imagine this. Only a complete idiot would act like this. Indeed all our "good" materialists and communists have acted like this and keep on acting in this way. And they are proud on how dull, ignorant and arrogant they are.

The problem is that these dimwits have gained control in our world and that normal people who follow the wisdom of their ancestors are perceived like idiots lost in the past, lost in stupidness. And today it is nearly the case that you must apologize for being a spiritual person, for knowing about God, for living a life in respect, responsibility and care, empathy for others. You nearly must apologize for being not a dark, dull and bad materialist. And the worst thing is when spiritual people are so brainwashed that they start to explain their spiritual practice in materialistic terms and ways. They apologize for shamanistic practice, for working with demons, gods, good and bad influences. They try to explain it as psychological phenomena. What kind of nonsense!

On the other hand nearly every psychotherapist makes already paranormal experiences in his education. Every day so many experiences are made from all kinds of people which show that materialism is nonsense but nearly no one talks about to keep his image and his job.

It is time to return to the source, to our roots, to integrate mankind back into the natural-divine order. We cannot pay the luxury of being separated from our true nature, from our origins as it means darkness and the death of mind and soul. It means the nemesis of the human civilization.

In fact we must liberate ourselves from the materialistic elements in society, from the dark and evil ones. We must find back to our strength and we have to withstand the evil claims of the dark elite. We must increase the light, the spiritual power which makes darkness vanish.

## THE HOLISTIC HEALING TREATMENT

Such a type of healing treatment is something very rare. It nearly does not exist. I will explain why and where the problems are. I recently had a client who had been suffering from strange pains in his shoulder for more than two years daily. His nerves there felt like lying open without any protection and so they were very sensible. So far no doctor was able to help him. They did all kinds of examinations but without any results. Due to "incidents" we got into contact and I told him that I do my best to help him. First of all I asked him a lot of questions concerning his personality, his family, his social situation, his business situation, his problems in life, his needs, wishes, his health problems and certainly everything which could be connected to the pain in his shoulder. So I talk a long comprehensive anamnesis to understand him and his problems as good as possible. Then we made our first hypnotic session to discover the causes of the symptoms. It turned out that the reason for his pain was located in his childhood where he suffered from the inability of his mother to show him love and care. During the session I was able to ensure him that his mother truly loves him but because of own wounds of soul she closed herself emotionally and so was not able to express her love for her son. (This was proved later in a conversation with his father.) So indeed his soul was wounded by the cool attitude of his mother in his childhood. Then we discovered also that the air conditioning system of his car has blown too much cool air on his shoulder throughout the years which supported the symptoms there. Here we have already the interesting analogy of coolness on the soul level and coolness on the material/energetic level – both caused pain. I did a lot of healing and clearing work in the rest of the hypnotic session and I integrated love, being loved and many more good feelings in his soul so that he felt really good and happy. After a few days the pain came back but not so strong and we talked about it to find the reasons. The problem was that he had great fears of losing love or beloved ones. He missed the confidence that everything is good and okay and the fear called back the pain. So uncertainty was the problem now and he hadn´t talked with his mother so far to clear and heal his relationship with her. In a second hypnotic session I have integrated the feeling of security and the knowledge that he is safe, that everything is good and that he will never lose love, the feeling of being loved. Additionally I installed a program for self-healing where every time he uses a special gesture all self- healing processes start automatically to make him recover on all three planes. And at last I have installed a possibility to block all pains immediately, also by using a special gesture. This gave him security and the ability to help himself every time he is in need. In a third hypnotic session I have optimized his management of life and work for more balance and happiness which he missed very much already. Things can be quite simple sometimes and so the ideas to go dancing with his wife and to delegate work for more spare time have helped much to restore the joy of life and the happiness he missed.

The main points here are that a treatment must take place on all planes, - on the mental plane, the astral (soul), the physical (body) and then also regarding life and business. A patient or client has to be treated as a whole with all aspects – thoughts, emotions, behavior, social life, work and in best case also the spiritual part and if the patient is not spiritual then at least to show how important it is to be a "good soul" living in harmony with yourself and others, doing good things, caring about others and so on.

I have described a holistic approach of healing treatment. In this example I also gave him advice for homeopathic treatment for cases where he can help himself easily, for coping with stress, for recovery, for healing his liver which suffered from too many pills (painkiller). I also showed him a breathing technique to restore vital energy and to get rid of exhausted energies. And at last I have gained a new friend in this world.

Now when you think of the diversity of healing treatments – tell me one holistic treatment like I have described. All different kinds of treatment are limited to the used technique or approach (only body or only mind or only soul or only energetic, etc.). From this understanding we have to ask for a holistic approach for real healing where the best techniques are combined for full and lasting success. When you have a client or a patient then you must get a complete picture of him and his life, you must advise him for changes in his life in his business, in his behavior, you must heal his mind, his history (karma), his soul with all wounds and his body and in best case you lead him back on the positive path, the spiritual path. It is a comprehensive work, a holistic work. Healing has to take place in all aspects and all planes. If it does not, symptoms will come back maybe in a different way.

And at last – when you think of the materialistic understanding of healing – can you see how poor it is? You go to a doctor and he gives you some pills. It is so simple and so poor.

So please – if you need a treatment or if you give treatments – do it as holistic as possible just because only this really helps and lasts. This approach regards the law of perfection.


## TRAVELING THROUGH TIME AND SPACE

At the moment I am reading a book about traveling through time and space from Johannes von Buttlar which is called "Supersurfing". He talks about mental traveling like Bardon would say. The interesting point is that he travels also into the past with his mental body to witness events of our history. It is like normal traveling in the presence. He is also able to perceive the thoughts in the mind of the people in the past. It must be really great. So in fact you can travel into the past to watch and experience everything which ever happened. Your intention is your guide. What you want to see is where you are going to travel in zero time.

The reading or perceiving of the past and of the future with clairvoyance and all other senses and also the experience of former incarnations in past life therapy is known but that you are able to move to such events with your mental body is something special (from my point of view) and not really common. So it is an interesting topic.

The technique is quite simple. You must relax your whole physical body like in a self-hypnosis and then shift your consciousness, your sensation and activity to the mental plane, into your mental body. When you feel yourself completely "transferred" or shifted in your mental body you can get out of your sleeping physical body. Certainly you can ask for help and guidance by sending a short request/prayer to the spiritual realms. Meditating with Laosa will be also helpful. She is a wonderful being and a master in traveling. Look for her in the evocation book of Bardon.

Again it shows that the mind is unlimited and that everything is possible. Have much fun!

## EPILOGUE

I have started with Daisy and I want to end with her. Daisy is the Maltese dog of a good friend of mine, a famous TV star in Romania for dog food. She is so lovely, pure joy. When I think of her I ask myself who among the human beings is able to express so much joy of life? Maybe only children and maybe those who live in harmony with nature. To see such an expression of joy, love and happiness is something special today. Most people are not able to show any form of joy or happiness as they have lost them. And if people smile they often express pain at the same time. Animals enjoy being naturally embedded in the great divine order. They are not fallen like we human beings. We should orientate us on these positive examples to learn again the right attitude towards life. In our performance-orientated society we have lost so much.

Dear reader, I wish you the experience of joy, happiness, love and fulfillment in life!

In love, light and service,

Ray del Sole

## CONTACT

Dear Reader,

if you like to contact me, please regard the following:

I can only provide answers for genuine spiritual seekers on the path – not for curiosity. Before you ask me try first to answer your question by own research as many questions of beginners and advanced students are already answered in my books and in the recommended spiritual literature.

Please respect that

- I have not much time for answering questions. I am very busy.
- I do not provide any magical help in any case. There are others who provide direct support.
- Everyone has to go through the spiritual training by himself as training means a deep transformation of your personality, - there is simply no alternative. Discipline in training will let you reach all aims. Practice makes perfect!
- I am not interested in joining any kinds of circles, secret societies, brotherhoods etc.
- I am a genuine servant of the eternal light and only responsible to God, not to any kind of limited religion or human interests.

Please contact me via email or join my community:

Mailto: raydelsole@yahoo.de

http://sol-network.ning.com/

Yours,

Ray del Sole

About the author:

I am an architect with special skills in management, eco-biology and economics. Recently I have made a complete education in hypnotherapy and past-life-therapy. Now I am working as a hypno-coach for life & business. I offer workshops for spiritual development. In my youth I have visited many foreign countries so that I got to know the beautiful diversity of cultures and people. I am a cosmopolitan and I feel at home especially in the south and the east of the world. I feel the old bonds of former incarnations to other countries, forms of old love and appreciation.

When I was a little child I have dedicated myself to the aim of understanding the world completely, how everything works. Today I would say – to understand God, man and creation, to gain real wisdom. So I started very early to study books about sciences, mysteries, religions, cultures, ancient history and spiritual teachings. Around the age of eighteen I began with the spiritual training system of Bardon. Indeed I chose this life to make as much spiritual progress as possible. And with this I will continue until I leave the material plane. For the future I have some spiritual, altruistic projects in mind. Let´s see what the coming years will bring.

Yours, Ray

# INDEX

2012 ................ 2, 69, 94, 124

abilities23, 24, 25, 26, 29, 33, 37, 43, 51, 56, 59, 61, 63, 65, 72, 76, 77, 78, 84, 85, 87, 95, 96, 97, 100, 109, 119, 123, 129, 130, 131, 135, 138, 158, 160

Abisheka ........................... 23

abishekas ........................ 105

abundance ....... 104, 157, 158

accounts ........................... 29

affirmation ....................... 28

aims9, 22, 23, 24, 26, 27, 28, 37, 38, 44, 46, 62, 63, 81, 103, 105, 119, 152, 169

air element 52, 135, 146, 151

Akasha24, 27, 28, 30, 33, 35, 36, 49, 50, 54, 59, 61, 68, 72, 91, 92, 96, 97, 102, 105, 115

Amitabha .......................... 34

animals52, 53, 54, 77, 78, 92, 93, 136

Arion ........................... 39, 40

Asuras .................. 15, 16, 72

autohypnosis ... 60, 73, 95, 96

autosuggestion28, 95, 107, 123, 128

awareness11, 28, 34, 43, 53, 65, 112, 113, 139, 146, 147, 152, 154

bad emotions ............. 62, 137

balance2, 18, 30, 31, 32, 37, 61, 71, 73, 91, 99, 103, 128, 137, 142, 146, 147, 164

Bardon2, 21, 22, 25, 26, 27, 28, 33, 34, 35, 38, 39, 43, 44, 48, 51, 56, 57, 85, 88, 89, 94, 96, 106, 109, 110, 111, 113, 114, 115, 116, 117, 118, 119, 121, 128, 131, 132, 137, 139, 146, 151, 158, 159, 166, 167, 170

battery ........................ 29, 75

Bengal ............................ 134

big egos .................... 21, 120

bija .................................. 48

Blavatsky ......................... 118

blockades36, 38, 60, 61, 68, 89, 92, 102, 104, 112, 113, 114, 123, 129

body19, 33, 39, 44, 48, 54, 58, 60, 61, 65, 68, 72, 76, 77, 87, 89, 92, 98, 106, 108, 110, 111, 112, 113, 116, 121, 129, 130, 135, 137, 151, 165, 166, 167

Bon Buddhism ................... 43

booster ....................... 94, 95

born magicians ................ 114

Brahma ............................ 48

brothers of darkness ......... 81

Buddhas ............................ 34

Buddhism ......... 44, 47, 51, 57

business18, 26, 49, 69, 74, 114, 149, 163, 165, 170

butterflies ......................... 53

Catholic Church ................ 16

chakra47, 53, 55, 86, 89, 90, 100, 102, 112, 113, 129, 135, 137, 153

chalice ....................142, 143

chaos.................... 15, 70, 71

character11, 22, 66, 67, 78, 84, 121, 124, 151

characteristics9, 24, 48, 65, 66, 67, 76, 77, 78, 96, 115, 116, 122, 127, 137, 138, 154

cheetahs........................... 53

children19, 66, 67, 93, 101, 144, 168

chimpanzees..................... 53

circle.............. 22, 23, 24, 133

civil wars........................... 70

clairsentience ..............33, 44

clairvoyance27, 33, 34, 44, 51, 86, 166

Clairvoyance ..................... 86

completeness30, 31, 32, 63, 126, 157

consumption...... 19, 156, 161

cosmic letter A.................. 52

countervalue .................... 20

Covert Hypnosis................ 84

creation30, 35, 36, 46, 51, 71, 72, 78, 81, 86, 87, 90, 94, 104, 119, 124, 136, 153, 154, 155, 157, 158, 170

crystal........ 75, 101, 102, 103

Daisy............................3, 168

Dalai Lama....................... 40

debts ........................20, 103

deceased ... 81, 123, 133, 144

delusion........................10, 11

dematerialization.............. 52

detours ............................44

direct knowledge.............100

discussion.........117, 120, 124

dissociation .....................133

divine consciousness12,   55, 75

divine garden .......... 100, 101

divine nature..39, 40, 73, 140

divine self.........139, 140, 142

doctor ............... 19, 163, 166

Dolphins...........................54

Dr. M. K.................... 39, 139

Durga ........................48, 49

eagle .................... 52, 53, 78

earth14, 17, 35, 47, 57, 89, 90, 92, 97, 101, 109, 111, 113, 138, 146, 147, 152, 153, 155

earth element .................146

ecological terror ................69

economics....18, 20, 161, 170

ecstasy .............................24

efficiency...........................20

Ego....................................53

egocentric ........................18

egoism ........................90, 91

elements30, 31, 54, 86, 111, 115, 120, 121, 151, 163

elite15, 18, 20, 122, 127, 156, 163

Elysian Fields.....................45

emotions24, 25, 26, 29, 55, 63, 68, 72, 87, 95, 133, 148, 165

emptiness .......................157

energetic atmosphere64, 144

energy channels  60, 134, 137

enlightenment24, 31, 35, 36, 117, 120, 153

entertainment .........117, 119

enthusiasm...................... 26

*equilibrium* ..................... 111

Eric Idle.........................40, 41

esoteric ....... 10, 43, 118, 124

eternal light ......... 71, 73, 169

Eucharist........................... 57

evil10, 11, 12, 15, 16, 18, 19, 20, 21, 43, 46, 73, 90, 98, 149, 162, 163

exercise25, 26, 33, 34, 44, 56, 57, 61, 62, 116, 120, 150, 151

experiment...................... 47

fairy tales.......................... 45

family29, 35, 49, 64, 66, 67, 68, 69, 98, 105, 110, 144, 145, 163

fate...........27, 38, 71, 99, 141

fish ................................. 54

forgiveness142, 143, 145, 146, 150, 153

formulation ................... 154

forum ............................ 118

Frabato............................ 39

free will ....................38, 159

fullness.............. 32, 157, 158

game ............................. 134

Gerald Celente.............92, 94

god39, 40, 47, 48, 49, 76, 77, 82, 88, 139, 140, 141

God3, 11, 12, 14, 15, 17, 22, 24, 30, 34, 35, 36, 40, 50, 53, 58, 63, 71, 73, 77, 79, 86, 94, 100, 103, 104, 117, 118, 120, 132, 133, 135,

136, 140, 146, 153, 154, 157, 159, 160, 162, 169, 170

goddess............45, 47, 48, 49

gold...................... 17, 30, 31

good and bad .... 46, 151, 162

Gottfried von Purucker....118

hara chakra ......................90

healing10, 35, 36, 51, 60, 61, 64, 68, 70, 89, 91, 92, 102, 103, 105, 112, 113, 123, 128, 129, 135, 136, 137, 138, 139, 140, 141, 142, 143, 144, 145, 146, 147, 148, 150, 152, 153, 163, 165, 166

health19, 29, 39, 61, 62, 88, 89, 90, 92, 97, 98, 112, 136, 144, 145, 147, 155, 163

hermetic path....................21

holistic treatment............165

homeopathic treatment ..165

hygiene ..................... 63, 141

hypnosis51, 66, 74, 84, 96, 97, 123, 131, 139, 141, 142, 143, 150, 152, 159, 167

hypnotherapy84, 131, 142, 170

hypnotic treatment77, 89, 96, 107, 124

ideal...............18, 19, 22, 115

imagination33, 34, 36, 43, 44, 50, 58, 64, 68, 74, 84, 85, 86, 87, 88, 89, 128, 129, 133, 134, 140, 143, 145

imbalance .......... 31, 71, 147

imitation...........................88

incarnation31, 37, 49, 67, 72, 73, 97, 99, 139, 143, 149, 150

incarnations2, 31, 32, 39, 103, 138, 140, 166, 170

information26, 39, 65, 105, 115, 117, 125, 129, 139, 152, 158

INHERITANCE .. 64, 65, 144, 160

internet forums .........38, 117

Jesus.........16, 17, 40, 76, 118

Johannes von Buttlar ...... 166

journalist .......................... 19

Kabbalah .................131, 133

karma11, 27, 28, 35, 36, 37, 38, 39, 46, 64, 71, 97, 99, 103, 104, 105, 110, 131, 137, 139, 141, 142, 143, 144, 146, 160, 165

karma yoga....................... 35

Kevin Hogan.................83, 84

kindergarten...................... 93

Krishna ............................. 49

KTQ ..........................132, 133

Kundalini .....................89, 90

Lakshmi ......................48, 49

Laosa .............................. 167

laughter.............. 40, 41, 117

law of silence................... 22

laws10, 11, 38, 46, 71, 72, 73, 118, 155

Learning .....................57, 59

lessons.............. 37, 141, 143

lessons of life.................... 37

lions.............................53, 78

love11, 12, 16, 21, 22, 31, 33, 35, 36, 37, 44, 49, 53, 58, 64, 74, 79, 91, 101, 108, 117, 124, 126, 135, 136, 137, 138, 140, 142, 143, 145, 146, 150, 153, 155, 156, 157, 161, 164, 168, 170

lunatic asylum16, 76, 92, 98, 122

macrocosm48, 73, 90, 115, 116, 139

magic21, 25, 26, 27, 28, 32, 33, 34, 44, 51, 55, 56, 57, 59, 74, 75, 76, 81, 82, 83, 85, 86, 94, 101, 106, 113, 119, 130, 133, 142

magical circle .................133

magical investments..........29

magical operations53, 74, 75, 121

Maha yoga ........................35

Mahdi ...............................69

Mammon .........17, 18, 19, 20

manifestation.57, 58, 85, 159

mankind12, 35, 40, 81, 86, 90, 92, 120, 122, 127, 153, 155, 156, 159, 160, 161, 163

Mantra Yoga......................24

mantras...... 47, 48, 49, 50, 51

master9, 23, 25, 26, 27, 28, 35, 37, 38, 39, 50, 52, 55, 58, 63, 71, 72, 73, 79, 80, 84, 86, 91, 94, 95, 103, 105, 111, 113, 114, 119, 120, 133, 138, 139, 160, 167 masters9, 27, 34, 56, 72, 76, 77, 81, 86, 103, 104, 117, 120, 121, 133, 139

mastership25, 26, 38, 56, 59, 83, 84, 85, 87, 117, 121, 135

Materialism .................... 126

materialization................. 52

maturity9, 23, 24, 38, 40, 100, 125, 159

meditation24, 25, 26, 29, 33, 43, 57, 74, 78, 85, 86, 95, 96, 107, 108, 116, 128, 129, 133, 137, 140, 151, 152

Messiah .......................... 69

Meta level ........................ 55

metaphysics...................... 71

microcosm48, 50, 60, 61, 64, 68, 75, 87, 90, 112, 115, 116, 129, 137, 153

Milan Ryzl ....................... 158

milestones............. 12, 26, 43

mind4, 10, 12, 19, 26, 31, 33, 34, 44, 53, 54, 60, 61, 65, 68, 74, 83, 88, 89, 96, 100, 106, 107, 109, 111, 112, 113, 116, 120, 130, 131, 134, 139, 145, 148, 156, 161, 163, 165, 166, 167, 170

mirroring .......................... 88

missionaries...................... 45

money17, 18, 19, 20, 21, 29, 84, 126, 150, 156, 161

Monty Python.................. 40

Mother Holle ................... 45

Muppet Show .................. 93

mysteries of love .............. 79

mystical wedding............. 140

nadis .............. 60, 61, 86, 137

negative connections. 68, 134

negative hierarchy..... 46, 104

Neptune........................... 54

Neuro-Programmer ........... 28

New World Order .............. 69

Nita Hickok...................... 105

objective level ................... 55

occult......................... 32, 51

opinion...................... 15, 125

order15, 32, 44, 70, 71, 72, 111, 128, 147, 157, 163, 168

Ouija ................................ 51

parapsychology ......... 51, 158

parasites ........... 64, 113, 133

patterns . 60, 63, 99, 145, 148

pendulum.......................... 51

perfection30, 31, 32, 35, 63, 73, 105, 114, 140, 166

performance39, 150, 151, 168

personal god ................... 139

personal point of view.......55

personality22, 29, 39, 54, 57, 65, 67, 68, 72, 78, 111, 118, 122, 123, 124, 127, 129, 130, 134, 137, 139, 141, 144, 147, 163, 169

pharmaceutical industry....19

philosophers ..................... 15

plan............................ 26, 59

Platon ............................. 27

politicians13, 14, 15, 16, 18, 20

poor18, 120, 149, 160, 161, 162, 166

Pope ................. 13, 14, 15, 16

positive hierarchy46, 103, 104

positivism .......................... 15

positivistic reason ........13, 14

power12, 15, 19, 29, 36, 48, 53, 58, 59, 60, 64, 66, 70, 71, 72, 74, 75, 76, 78, 90, 95, 96, 97, 109, 110, 113, 121, 127, 137, 140, 142, 146, 150, 163

Pranic Healers .................... 43

problems21, 36, 39, 55, 57, 61, 62, 64, 65, 67, 72, 76, 84, 88, 97, 98, 99, 107, 112, 126, 127, 132, 134, 136, 138, 139, 141, 143, 144, 145, 147, 149, 150, 152, 155, 163

Process imagination .......... 85

proclamation ... 103, 104, 105

programming ...........148, 150

progress9, 12, 36, 40, 43, 45, 55, 58, 59, 62, 79, 85, 95, 97, 103, 104, 105, 114, 115, 117, 121, 123, 149, 154, 170

protection29, 49, 101, 104, 125, 163

psychology ..... 51, 83, 88, 111

psychopaths92, 94, 122, 127, 138

psychotherapy10, 51, 76, 77, 126

punishment ..... 17, 46, 70, 73

puzzle ............................. 125

Quabbalah .............. 121, 132

Quabbalist ........... 17, 91, 136

radiance ............ 75, 137, 153

reality23, 25, 51, 66, 70, 72, 77, 82, 85, 86, 87, 117, 130

regression ................ 84, 150

Reiki ................................44

remedy ...........................136

resonance .... 67, 88, 116, 136

resources ............ 76, 78, 105

result imagination .............85

rich ..................... 17, 18, 149

rituals.................... 24, 81, 96

Rosecrucians .....................16

Rudolf Steiner .................118

salt bath..........................113

Saraswati ..........................48

Satanists69, 70, 72, 73, 122, 160

Satsang .............................23

saturation ............. 30, 31, 32

science2, 15, 18, 51, 71, 83, 109, 126, 161

Scientists.....................18, 70

scissors...........................134

secrets societies ...............11

seeds27, 28, 37, 79, 95, 99, 143, 144

seeds of karma .................27

seeker9, 11, 12, 83, 94, 95, 139

self-clearing................60, 61

self-confidence...... 53, 77, 78

self-determination66, 68, 133, 136

self-esteem .......................53

self-influence ...................28

servants of darkness..........15

servants of light ................ 81
Shakti ......................... 89, 90
Shamans ........................... 77
shields ........................... 134
shift of consciousness ..... 107
Shiva ........................ 48, 110
sociopaths ... 92, 94, 122, 127
solar system ............. 111, 116
soul 10, 11, 19, 23, 31, 50, 54, 60, 61, 65, 68, 83, 89, 91, 106, 121, 123, 141, 142, 143, 144, 145, 151, 156, 161, 163, 164, 165
soul mirror work ............... 23
sparrows ......................... 52
spheres ............ 115, 116, 139
spiritual development 21, 44, 49, 73, 83, 84, 85, 94, 95, 97, 103, 105, 114, 115, 118, 119, 131, 138, 139, 141, 146, 152, 154, 156, 170
spiritual evolution ............ 37
spiritual guide 79, 123, 130, 139, 141, 152, 153, 154
spiritual leaders .......... 10, 11
spiritual master 35, 38, 39, 55
spiritual people 31, 36, 158, 162
static state ....................... 30
stress 56, 80, 88, 89, 108, 135, 165
structure 22, 29, 30, 39, 58, 76, 115, 156
study groups ..................... 21
subconsciousness 28, 58, 60, 61, 66, 73, 83, 85, 86, 95, 96, 97, 106, 123

success 22, 27, 29, 34, 36, 56, 57, 58, 59, 104, 114, 154, 165
sunlight 16, 102, 130, 155, 156
super-personal ................. 55
Taoistic Alchemy .............. 44
target-state .................... 128
Tarot Card ...................... 140
Teachings ......................... 12
telepathy .......... 33, 34, 44, 52
tension ............. 56, 75, 76, 89
terrorists ......................... 70
the perfect worker ............ 19
third eye .......................... 86
third world war ................. 69
tigers .......................... 53, 78
tourmaline ............. 101, 102
traditional magic ............ 119
training 2, 10, 22, 23, 24, 26, 31, 34, 38, 39, 40, 43, 44, 46, 53, 56, 57, 58, 59, 62, 63, 66, 75, 84, 85, 87, 94, 95, 96, 97, 100, 104, 106, 107, 108, 109, 110, 113, 114, 115, 116, 120, 123, 124, 127, 128, 130, 132, 134, 140, 154, 158, 169, 170
trance 61, 73, 106, 107, 108, 109, 123, 130, 131, 133, 140, 152
transformation 39, 58, 77, 169
traps .................... 10, 12, 43
treatments 51, 68, 69, 113, 114, 123, 143, 144, 165, 166

triggers ............................. 96
true spiritual attitude...22, 44
Udo Ulfkotte..................... 94
Venus .............................. 54
virtues12, 22, 25, 26, 31, 73,
    75, 77, 140
virus ................................ 70
Vishnu ........................48, 49
vow ................. 103, 105, 150
water element ...........54, 111
whales.............................. 54

William Mistele32, 33, 43,
    109
wire dancer .................... 9, 12
wisdom10, 12, 22, 31, 74,
    118, 140, 155, 156, 160,
    162, 170
wishes25, 29, 37, 38, 48, 49,
    54, 72, 75, 99, 102, 152,
    156, 163
Yoga............... 24, 35, 57, 138
youtube ...........................50

Made in the USA
Lexington, KY
26 November 2013